# 50 Rhubarb Recipes for Home

By: Kelly Johnson

# Table of Contents

**Pies:**

- Rhubarb Pie
- Rhubarb Crisp
- Rhubarb Custard Pie
- Rhubarb Strawberry Jam
- Rhubarb Chutney
- Rhubarb Lemonade
- Rhubarb Cake
- Rhubarb Muffins
- Rhubarb Bars
- Rhubarb Compote
- Rhubarb Cobbler
- Rhubarb Bread
- Rhubarb Sauce
- Rhubarb Ice Cream
- Rhubarb Tart
- Rhubarb Scones
- Rhubarb Jelly
- Rhubarb Punch
- Rhubarb Cookies
- Rhubarb Crumble
- Rhubarb Pancakes
- Rhubarb Upside-Down Cake
- Rhubarb Vinaigrette
- Rhubarb Margarita
- Rhubarb BBQ Sauce
- Rhubarb Trifle
- Rhubarb Syrup
- Rhubarb Smoothie
- Rhubarb Popsicles
- Rhubarb Cheesecake
- Rhubarb Relish
- Rhubarb Compote
- Rhubarb Slush

- Rhubarb Wine
- Rhubarb Glaze
- Rhubarb Shortcake
- Rhubarb Chiffon Pie
- Rhubarb Breakfast Bars
- Rhubarb Daiquiri
- Rhubarb Salad Dressing
- Rhubarb Marinade
- Rhubarb Custard Bars
- Rhubarb Lemon Bars
- Rhubarb Butter
- Rhubarb Crisp Bars
- Rhubarb Baked Beans
- Rhubarb Coffee Cake
- Rhubarb Whiskey Sour
- Rhubarb Fritters
- Rhubarb Cinnamon Rolls

**Rhubarb Pie**

Ingredients:

- 4 cups rhubarb, sliced into 1-inch pieces
- 1 1/4 cups granulated sugar
- 1/4 cup all-purpose flour
- 1/2 teaspoon ground cinnamon
- 1/4 teaspoon ground nutmeg
- 1 tablespoon butter, cut into small pieces
- 2 (9-inch) pie crusts (homemade or store-bought)

Instructions:

Prepare the Oven:

Preheat your oven to 425°F (220°C).

Prepare the Rhubarb:

Wash the rhubarb stalks and slice them into 1-inch pieces.

Mix the Filling:

In a large bowl, combine the sliced rhubarb, sugar, flour, cinnamon, and nutmeg. Toss everything together until the rhubarb is evenly coated.

Prepare the Pie Crust:

Roll out one of the pie crusts and line a 9-inch pie dish with it.

Fill the Pie:

Pour the rhubarb filling into the pie crust, spreading it out evenly. Dot the top of the filling with small pieces of butter.

Cover the Pie:

Roll out the second pie crust and place it over the filling. Trim any excess crust from the edges and crimp the edges together to seal the pie. You can also flute the edges decoratively.

Vent the Pie:

Use a sharp knife to make several small slits in the top crust. This will allow steam to escape while baking.

Bake the Pie:

Place the pie in the preheated oven and bake for 15 minutes. Then reduce the oven temperature to 350°F (175°C) and continue baking for an additional 40-45 minutes, or until the crust is golden brown and the filling is bubbly.

Cool and Serve:

Once baked, remove the pie from the oven and let it cool on a wire rack before slicing and serving. Serve warm or at room temperature, optionally with a scoop of vanilla ice cream or a dollop of whipped cream.

Enjoy your homemade rhubarb pie! Adjust the sweetness according to your taste preference, as the tartness of rhubarb can vary. This pie is a wonderful way to enjoy the unique flavor of fresh rhubarb when it's in season.

**Rhubarb Crisp**

Ingredients:

For the Filling:

- 4 cups rhubarb, chopped into 1-inch pieces
- 1 cup granulated sugar
- 2 tablespoons all-purpose flour
- 1 teaspoon vanilla extract

For the Crisp Topping:

- 1 cup old-fashioned rolled oats
- 1/2 cup all-purpose flour
- 1/2 cup packed brown sugar
- 1/2 teaspoon ground cinnamon
- 1/4 teaspoon salt
- 1/2 cup unsalted butter, cold and cut into small pieces

Instructions:

Preheat the Oven:

Preheat your oven to 350°F (175°C).

Prepare the Rhubarb Filling:

In a large bowl, combine the chopped rhubarb, granulated sugar, flour, and vanilla extract. Toss until the rhubarb is coated evenly with the sugar mixture. Transfer this mixture into a 9x9-inch baking dish or a similar-sized baking dish.

Make the Crisp Topping:

In another bowl, mix together the rolled oats, flour, brown sugar, cinnamon, and salt. Add the cold butter pieces to the mixture and use a pastry cutter, fork, or your fingers to combine everything until it resembles coarse crumbs.

Assemble and Bake:

Sprinkle the crisp topping evenly over the rhubarb filling in the baking dish.

Bake the Crisp:

Place the baking dish in the preheated oven and bake for 40-45 minutes, or until the topping is golden brown and the filling is bubbly.

Serve:

Remove the rhubarb crisp from the oven and let it cool slightly. Serve warm, either on its own or with a scoop of vanilla ice cream or a dollop of whipped cream.

Enjoy this delicious rhubarb crisp, with its contrasting textures of tender rhubarb and crunchy oat topping. It's a perfect dessert for showcasing the flavors of spring and early summer when rhubarb is in season. Adjust the sweetness of the filling according to your preference, especially if you prefer a more or less tart dessert.

## Rhubarb Custard Pie

Ingredients:

For the Pie Crust:

- 1 ½ cups all-purpose flour
- ½ teaspoon salt
- ½ cup unsalted butter, chilled and cubed
- 4-6 tablespoons ice water

For the Filling:

- 3 cups diced rhubarb (about ½-inch pieces)
- 1 ½ cups granulated sugar
- 4 large eggs
- ¼ cup all-purpose flour
- ½ teaspoon ground nutmeg
- ½ teaspoon vanilla extract
- Whipped cream or vanilla ice cream (for serving, optional)

Instructions:

Prepare the Pie Crust:
- In a large mixing bowl, combine the flour and salt.
- Add the chilled, cubed butter to the flour mixture.
- Use a pastry cutter or fork to cut the butter into the flour until the mixture resembles coarse crumbs.
- Gradually add ice water, 1 tablespoon at a time, mixing with a fork until the dough starts to come together.
- Gather the dough into a ball, flatten into a disc, wrap in plastic wrap, and refrigerate for at least 30 minutes.

Preheat the Oven:
- Preheat your oven to 400°F (200°C).

Roll out the Pie Crust:
- On a lightly floured surface, roll out the chilled pie dough into a circle large enough to line a 9-inch pie dish. Transfer the dough to the pie dish, trim any excess dough, and crimp the edges decoratively. Place the pie crust in the refrigerator while you prepare the filling.

Prepare the Rhubarb Filling:
- In a large bowl, combine the diced rhubarb and granulated sugar. Let this mixture sit for about 15 minutes to allow the rhubarb to release some of its juices.

- In another bowl, whisk together the eggs, flour, nutmeg, and vanilla extract until smooth.

Assemble the Pie:
- Drain any excess liquid from the rhubarb mixture.
- Spread the rhubarb evenly over the bottom of the chilled pie crust.
- Pour the egg mixture over the rhubarb, ensuring that it is evenly distributed.

Bake the Pie:
- Place the pie in the preheated oven and bake for 10 minutes.
- Reduce the oven temperature to 350°F (175°C) and continue baking for another 35-40 minutes, or until the custard is set and the top is golden brown.

Cool and Serve:
- Remove the pie from the oven and let it cool completely on a wire rack.
- Serve the rhubarb custard pie at room temperature, optionally topped with whipped cream or vanilla ice cream.

Enjoy this delicious rhubarb custard pie, with its smooth custard filling complementing the tangy rhubarb. It's a perfect dessert for rhubarb lovers and a delightful treat during rhubarb season! Adjust the sweetness according to your taste preference, especially if you prefer a sweeter or more tart pie.

**Rhubarb Strawberry Jam**

Ingredients:

- 4 cups diced rhubarb (about 1/2-inch pieces)
- 4 cups strawberries, hulled and chopped
- 5 cups granulated sugar
- 1/4 cup lemon juice (freshly squeezed)
- 1 package (1.75 oz) powdered fruit pectin (such as Sure-Jell)

Instructions:

Prepare the Fruit:
- Wash the rhubarb stalks and strawberries thoroughly.
- Dice the rhubarb into small pieces (about 1/2 inch) and chop the strawberries.

Combine Ingredients:
- In a large pot or preserving pan, combine the diced rhubarb, chopped strawberries, granulated sugar, and lemon juice. Mix well.

Let the Fruit Macerate:
- Let the fruit mixture sit for about 1-2 hours at room temperature. This helps the sugar to draw out the juices from the fruit.

Prepare for Cooking:
- After macerating, stir the fruit mixture and bring it to a simmer over medium-high heat.

Add Pectin:
- Once the fruit mixture is simmering, stir in the powdered fruit pectin. Mix well to ensure the pectin is fully incorporated.

Cook the Jam:
- Continue to cook the jam mixture over medium-high heat, stirring frequently to prevent sticking and burning.
- Cook until the jam thickens and reaches the desired consistency. This can take about 15-20 minutes.

Test for Doneness:
- To test if the jam is ready, place a small amount on a chilled plate. Allow it to cool for a minute. If it wrinkles when nudged with a finger, it's done. If not, continue cooking and re-test.

Can the Jam:
- While the jam is cooking, prepare your canning jars and lids by sterilizing them in boiling water.

- Once the jam reaches the desired consistency, carefully ladle it into the sterilized jars, leaving a 1/4-inch headspace.
- Wipe the jar rims clean with a damp cloth, then place the lids and rings on the jars.

Process the Jars:
- Process the filled jars in a boiling water bath for 10-15 minutes to ensure proper sealing and preservation.

Cool and Store:
- After processing, remove the jars from the water bath and let them cool completely at room temperature.
- Check that the jars are properly sealed (the lids should be concave and not springy when pressed).
- Label the jars with the jam type and date before storing them in a cool, dark place.

Enjoy:
- Once cooled and sealed, your rhubarb strawberry jam is ready to enjoy! Spread it on toast, use it as a topping for yogurt or ice cream, or give it as a homemade gift.

This rhubarb strawberry jam will bring a taste of summer to your table and can be enjoyed throughout the year. Experiment with the sugar amount based on your sweetness preference and the tartness of your rhubarb and strawberries.

**Rhubarb Chutney**

Ingredients:

- 4 cups diced rhubarb (about 1/2-inch pieces)
- 1 cup chopped onion
- 1 cup dried cranberries or raisins
- 1 cup packed brown sugar
- 1 cup apple cider vinegar
- 1 tablespoon grated fresh ginger
- 1 teaspoon mustard seeds
- 1/2 teaspoon ground cinnamon
- 1/2 teaspoon ground cloves
- 1/2 teaspoon salt
- 1/4 teaspoon cayenne pepper (optional, for a bit of heat)
- Zest and juice of 1 orange

Instructions:

Prepare the Ingredients:
- Wash the rhubarb stalks and dice them into small pieces (about 1/2 inch). Chop the onion and grate the fresh ginger.

Combine Ingredients in a Pot:
- In a large, heavy-bottomed pot, combine the diced rhubarb, chopped onion, dried cranberries or raisins, brown sugar, apple cider vinegar, grated ginger, mustard seeds, ground cinnamon, ground cloves, salt, and cayenne pepper (if using).
- Stir well to combine all ingredients.

Cook the Chutney:
- Place the pot over medium-high heat and bring the mixture to a boil, stirring frequently.
- Once boiling, reduce the heat to low and let the chutney simmer gently for about 30-40 minutes, or until the rhubarb is tender and the mixture has thickened to a chutney-like consistency. Stir occasionally to prevent sticking.

Add Orange Zest and Juice:
- Once the chutney has thickened, stir in the zest and juice of one orange. This will add brightness and depth of flavor to the chutney.

Adjust Seasonings:

- Taste the chutney and adjust the seasonings to your preference. You can add more sugar if you prefer a sweeter chutney, or more salt and spices for extra flavor.

Cool and Store:
- Remove the pot from the heat and let the rhubarb chutney cool to room temperature.
- Transfer the chutney into clean, sterilized jars. Seal the jars tightly and store them in the refrigerator.

Serve and Enjoy:
- Rhubarb chutney is best served chilled or at room temperature.
- Enjoy this tangy and flavorful chutney as a condiment with grilled meats, roasted vegetables, cheeses, sandwiches, or even as a topping for crackers or crostini.

This rhubarb chutney will keep well in the refrigerator for several weeks. The flavors will continue to develop over time, making it even more delicious as it matures. Experiment with this recipe by adjusting the sweetness and spices to suit your taste preferences.

**Rhubarb Lemonade**

Ingredients:

- 4 cups chopped rhubarb (about 1/2-inch pieces)
- 1 cup granulated sugar (adjust based on desired sweetness)
- 6 cups water
- Zest and juice of 2-3 lemons (about 1/2 cup lemon juice)
- Ice cubes
- Fresh mint leaves (for garnish, optional)

Instructions:

Prepare the Rhubarb:
- Wash the rhubarb stalks thoroughly and chop them into small pieces (about 1/2 inch).

Cook the Rhubarb Syrup:
- In a large pot, combine the chopped rhubarb, granulated sugar, and water.
- Bring the mixture to a boil over medium-high heat, then reduce the heat to low and let it simmer for about 15-20 minutes, or until the rhubarb is very soft and breaks down.

Strain the Rhubarb Mixture:
- Once the rhubarb has cooked down, remove the pot from the heat.
- Place a fine-mesh sieve or cheesecloth over a large bowl or pitcher.
- Pour the rhubarb mixture through the sieve or cheesecloth to strain out the solids, pressing down gently to extract all the liquid.
- Discard the solids and allow the rhubarb syrup to cool to room temperature.

Add Lemon Juice and Zest:
- Once the rhubarb syrup has cooled, stir in the freshly squeezed lemon juice and zest.
- Taste the mixture and adjust the sweetness or tartness by adding more sugar or lemon juice, if desired.

Chill the Lemonade:
- Refrigerate the rhubarb lemonade until well chilled, about 1-2 hours.

Serve:
- Fill glasses with ice cubes.
- Pour the chilled rhubarb lemonade over the ice cubes.
- Garnish with fresh mint leaves, if desired.

Enjoy:

- Stir the rhubarb lemonade before serving to distribute the flavors.
- Sip and enjoy this delightful and tangy rhubarb lemonade on a hot day!

You can also customize this rhubarb lemonade by adding sparkling water for a fizzy version or mixing in other fruits like strawberries or raspberries for added flavor. Experiment with the sweetness and tartness levels to suit your taste preferences. This homemade rhubarb lemonade is a perfect balance of sweet, tart, and refreshing flavors!

**Rhubarb Cake**

Ingredients:

- 2 cups diced rhubarb (about 1/2-inch pieces)
- 1 1/2 cups granulated sugar, divided
- 1/2 cup unsalted butter, softened
- 1 egg
- 1 teaspoon vanilla extract
- 2 cups all-purpose flour
- 1 teaspoon baking powder
- 1/2 teaspoon baking soda
- 1/4 teaspoon salt
- 1 cup buttermilk (or substitute with 1 cup milk mixed with 1 tablespoon lemon juice or vinegar)

For the Topping:

- 1/4 cup granulated sugar
- 1 teaspoon ground cinnamon

Instructions:

Preheat the Oven and Prepare the Pan:
- Preheat your oven to 350°F (175°C).
- Grease and flour a 9x13-inch baking dish or a similar-sized cake pan.

Prepare the Rhubarb:
- Wash the rhubarb stalks and dice them into small pieces (about 1/2 inch). Toss the diced rhubarb with 1/2 cup of granulated sugar and set aside.

Make the Cake Batter:
- In a large mixing bowl, cream together the softened butter and remaining 1 cup of granulated sugar until light and fluffy.
- Add the egg and vanilla extract to the butter-sugar mixture, and beat until well combined.

Combine Dry Ingredients:
- In a separate bowl, whisk together the flour, baking powder, baking soda, and salt.

Alternate Adding Ingredients:
- Gradually add the dry ingredients to the butter-sugar mixture, alternating with buttermilk. Begin and end with the dry ingredients.

- Mix until just combined. Do not overmix.

Fold in Rhubarb:
- Gently fold the diced rhubarb (along with any accumulated juices) into the cake batter.

Pour Batter into Pan:
- Spread the cake batter evenly into the prepared baking dish.

Make the Topping:
- In a small bowl, mix together the 1/4 cup of granulated sugar and ground cinnamon.
- Sprinkle the cinnamon sugar mixture evenly over the top of the cake batter.

Bake the Cake:
- Place the cake in the preheated oven and bake for 40-45 minutes, or until a toothpick inserted into the center comes out clean and the top is golden brown.

Cool and Serve:
- Remove the cake from the oven and let it cool in the pan for about 10-15 minutes.
- Serve the rhubarb cake warm or at room temperature.
- Optionally, you can dust the top with powdered sugar before serving.

Enjoy this delicious rhubarb cake as a dessert or a sweet treat with coffee or tea. The tangy rhubarb adds a wonderful flavor and texture to this moist and flavorful cake. Store any leftovers in an airtight container at room temperature for up to a few days.

**Rhubarb Muffins**

Ingredients:

- 2 cups all-purpose flour
- 1 cup granulated sugar
- 2 teaspoons baking powder
- 1/2 teaspoon baking soda
- 1/2 teaspoon salt
- 1/2 cup unsalted butter, melted and cooled
- 1 cup buttermilk (or substitute with 1 cup milk mixed with 1 tablespoon lemon juice or vinegar)
- 2 large eggs
- 1 teaspoon vanilla extract
- 1 1/2 cups diced rhubarb (fresh or frozen)
- Optional: Turbinado sugar for sprinkling on top

Instructions:

Preheat the Oven and Prepare the Muffin Pan:

- Preheat your oven to 375°F (190°C).
- Line a 12-cup muffin pan with paper liners or grease each cup with butter or non-stick cooking spray.

Prepare the Dry Ingredients:

- In a large mixing bowl, whisk together the flour, sugar, baking powder, baking soda, and salt until well combined.

Prepare the Wet Ingredients:

- In another bowl, whisk together the melted butter, buttermilk, eggs, and vanilla extract until smooth.

Combine Wet and Dry Ingredients:

- Pour the wet ingredients into the bowl of dry ingredients.
- Gently fold and stir the mixture until just combined. Do not overmix; the batter should be lumpy.

Fold in Rhubarb:

- Gently fold the diced rhubarb into the muffin batter. Be careful not to overmix to avoid crushing the rhubarb pieces.

Fill Muffin Cups:

- Divide the muffin batter evenly among the prepared muffin cups, filling each cup about 2/3 full.

Optional: Sprinkle with Turbinado Sugar:

- For a crunchy topping, sprinkle a little bit of turbinado sugar over the tops of the muffins before baking.

Bake the Muffins:

- Place the muffin pan in the preheated oven and bake for 18-20 minutes, or until the muffins are golden brown and a toothpick inserted into the center comes out clean.

Cool and Serve:

- Remove the muffins from the oven and let them cool in the pan for a few minutes.
- Transfer the muffins to a wire rack to cool completely before serving.

Enjoy these delicious rhubarb muffins for breakfast, as a snack, or with a cup of tea or coffee. Store any leftover muffins in an airtight container at room temperature for a few days, or freeze them for longer storage. The tart rhubarb provides a burst of flavor in every bite of these moist and tender muffins! Adjust the sweetness to your liking by increasing or decreasing the amount of sugar in the recipe.

**Rhubarb Bars**

Ingredients:

For the Crust and Topping:

- 1 cup unsalted butter, softened
- 2 cups all-purpose flour
- 1/2 cup granulated sugar
- 1/4 teaspoon salt

For the Rhubarb Filling:

- 4 cups diced rhubarb (about 1/2-inch pieces)
- 1 1/2 cups granulated sugar
- 1/4 cup cornstarch
- 1/2 teaspoon vanilla extract

Instructions:

Preheat the Oven and Prepare the Pan:
- Preheat your oven to 350°F (175°C).
- Grease a 9x13-inch baking dish or line it with parchment paper.

Make the Crust and Topping:
- In a large mixing bowl, cream together the softened butter, flour, sugar, and salt until crumbly.
- Reserve about 1 1/2 cups of the mixture for the topping. Press the remaining mixture evenly into the bottom of the prepared baking dish to form the crust.

Prepare the Rhubarb Filling:
- In another bowl, combine the diced rhubarb, granulated sugar, cornstarch, and vanilla extract. Mix well to coat the rhubarb evenly.

Assemble the Bars:
- Spread the rhubarb filling over the crust in the baking dish, spreading it out evenly.

Add the Topping:
- Sprinkle the reserved crumb mixture evenly over the rhubarb filling to form the topping.

Bake the Bars:

- Place the baking dish in the preheated oven and bake for 45-50 minutes, or until the top is golden brown and the rhubarb filling is bubbly.

Cool and Serve:
- Remove the rhubarb bars from the oven and let them cool completely in the baking dish on a wire rack.
- Once cooled, use a sharp knife to cut the bars into squares or rectangles.

Serve and Enjoy:
- Serve the rhubarb bars at room temperature.
- Optionally, dust the bars with powdered sugar before serving for a decorative touch.

These rhubarb bars are perfect for any occasion and can be enjoyed as a delicious dessert or snack. The buttery crust pairs beautifully with the tart rhubarb filling, making these bars a crowd-pleaser. Store any leftover bars in an airtight container at room temperature for a few days, or refrigerate them for longer storage. Enjoy the wonderful flavors of rhubarb in these delightful bars! Adjust the sweetness of the filling according to your preference, especially if you prefer a more or less tart dessert.

**Rhubarb Compote**

Ingredients:

- 4 cups diced rhubarb (about 1/2-inch pieces)
- 1/2 cup granulated sugar (adjust to taste depending on tartness of rhubarb)
- Zest and juice of 1 orange (or lemon)
- 1 cinnamon stick (optional)
- 1/2 teaspoon vanilla extract (optional)
- Pinch of salt
- Water (as needed)

Instructions:

Prepare the Rhubarb:
- Wash the rhubarb stalks and dice them into small pieces (about 1/2 inch).

Cook the Rhubarb:
- In a medium saucepan, combine the diced rhubarb, granulated sugar, orange zest, orange juice, cinnamon stick (if using), vanilla extract (if using), and a pinch of salt.
- Add a splash of water (about 1/4 cup) to the saucepan to prevent sticking and help the rhubarb release its juices.

Simmer the Mixture:
- Place the saucepan over medium heat and bring the mixture to a gentle simmer, stirring occasionally.
- Reduce the heat to low and let the rhubarb cook gently for about 10-15 minutes, or until the rhubarb is soft and begins to break down, stirring occasionally.

Adjust Sweetness and Flavor:
- Taste the compote and adjust the sweetness by adding more sugar if desired.
- If using a cinnamon stick, remove it from the compote once the desired flavor has been achieved.

Cool and Serve:
- Remove the saucepan from the heat and let the rhubarb compote cool slightly.
- Serve the compote warm or chill it in the refrigerator before serving.

Storage:
- Store any leftover rhubarb compote in a sealed container in the refrigerator for up to a week.

Serving Suggestions:

- Serve warm rhubarb compote over vanilla ice cream or Greek yogurt.
- Enjoy chilled rhubarb compote as a topping for oatmeal, pancakes, waffles, or French toast.
- Use rhubarb compote as a filling for pies, tarts, or pastries.
- Swirl rhubarb compote into muffin or cake batters for added flavor.

This rhubarb compote recipe is customizable based on your preferences. Feel free to adjust the sweetness and add different spices or flavorings to suit your taste. Rhubarb compote is a delightful way to enjoy the unique flavor of rhubarb and can be used in a variety of sweet dishes or enjoyed simply on its own.

**Rhubarb Cobbler**

Ingredients:

For the Rhubarb Filling:

- 5 cups diced rhubarb (about 1/2-inch pieces)
- 1 cup granulated sugar
- 2 tablespoons cornstarch
- 1 teaspoon vanilla extract
- Zest and juice of 1 orange (optional)

For the Cobbler Topping:

- 1 1/2 cups all-purpose flour
- 1/2 cup granulated sugar
- 1 1/2 teaspoons baking powder
- 1/2 teaspoon salt
- 1/2 cup unsalted butter, cold and cubed
- 2/3 cup buttermilk (or substitute with regular milk)
- Optional: Turbinado sugar, for sprinkling

Instructions:

Preheat the Oven:
- Preheat your oven to 375°F (190°C).

Prepare the Rhubarb Filling:
- In a large bowl, combine the diced rhubarb, granulated sugar, cornstarch, vanilla extract, and orange zest/juice (if using). Mix well to coat the rhubarb evenly.

Transfer to Baking Dish:
- Transfer the rhubarb mixture into a 9x13-inch baking dish or similar-sized casserole dish, spreading it out evenly.

Make the Cobbler Topping:
- In a separate bowl, whisk together the flour, sugar, baking powder, and salt.
- Add the cold, cubed butter to the flour mixture. Use a pastry cutter, fork, or your fingers to cut the butter into the flour until the mixture resembles coarse crumbs.

- Gradually pour in the buttermilk, mixing with a fork until just combined. The dough should be moist and slightly sticky.

Assemble the Cobbler:
- Drop spoonfuls of the cobbler dough evenly over the rhubarb filling in the baking dish, covering most of the surface.

Bake the Cobbler:
- Place the baking dish in the preheated oven and bake for 40-45 minutes, or until the cobbler topping is golden brown and the rhubarb filling is bubbling underneath.

Cool and Serve:
- Remove the rhubarb cobbler from the oven and let it cool for a few minutes before serving.
- Optionally, sprinkle the top of the cobbler with turbinado sugar for added sweetness and crunch.

Serve and Enjoy:
- Serve the rhubarb cobbler warm, optionally topped with vanilla ice cream or whipped cream.
- Store any leftover cobbler in the refrigerator and reheat before serving.

Enjoy this delicious rhubarb cobbler, with its tender and sweet biscuit-like topping contrasting beautifully with the tangy rhubarb filling. Adjust the sweetness of the filling according to your preference, especially if you prefer a sweeter or more tart cobbler. This dessert is perfect for showcasing the wonderful flavors of fresh rhubarb in a comforting and satisfying dish!

**Rhubarb Bread**

Ingredients:

- 1 1/2 cups diced rhubarb (about 1/2-inch pieces)
- 1 1/2 cups granulated sugar
- 1/2 cup vegetable oil
- 1 egg
- 1 teaspoon vanilla extract
- 1 cup buttermilk (or substitute with 1 cup milk mixed with 1 tablespoon lemon juice or vinegar)
- 2 1/2 cups all-purpose flour
- 1 teaspoon baking soda
- 1/2 teaspoon baking powder
- 1/2 teaspoon salt
- 1/2 cup chopped nuts (such as walnuts or pecans), optional
- Optional: Cinnamon sugar for sprinkling on top

Instructions:

Preheat the Oven and Prepare the Pan:
- Preheat your oven to 350°F (175°C).
- Grease and flour a 9x5-inch loaf pan.

Prepare the Rhubarb:
- Wash the rhubarb stalks and dice them into small pieces (about 1/2 inch).

Mix Wet Ingredients:
- In a large mixing bowl, combine the diced rhubarb, granulated sugar, vegetable oil, egg, vanilla extract, and buttermilk. Mix well.

Combine Dry Ingredients:
- In another bowl, whisk together the flour, baking soda, baking powder, and salt.

Combine Wet and Dry Ingredients:
- Gradually add the dry ingredients to the wet ingredients, stirring until just combined.
- If using nuts, fold them into the batter.

Bake the Bread:
- Pour the batter into the prepared loaf pan, spreading it out evenly.
- Optionally, sprinkle cinnamon sugar over the top of the batter for a sweet crust.

Bake the Bread:

- Place the loaf pan in the preheated oven and bake for 50-60 minutes, or until a toothpick inserted into the center comes out clean.

Cool and Serve:
- Remove the rhubarb bread from the oven and let it cool in the pan for about 10 minutes.
- Transfer the bread to a wire rack to cool completely before slicing.

Serve and Enjoy:
- Slice the rhubarb bread and serve it warm or at room temperature.
- This bread is delicious on its own or spread with butter or cream cheese.

Enjoy this homemade rhubarb bread as a delightful snack or dessert. The combination of sweet rhubarb and moist bread makes it a perfect treat for showcasing the flavors of spring and early summer. Store any leftover bread in an airtight container at room temperature for a few days, or freeze slices for longer storage.

**Rhubarb Sauce**

Ingredients:

- 4 cups diced rhubarb (about 1/2-inch pieces)
- 1 cup granulated sugar (adjust to taste depending on tartness of rhubarb)
- Zest and juice of 1 orange (or lemon)
- 1/2 teaspoon vanilla extract (optional)
- Pinch of ground cinnamon or cardamom (optional)
- 1/4 cup water

Instructions:

Prepare the Rhubarb:
- Wash the rhubarb stalks and dice them into small pieces (about 1/2 inch).

Cook the Rhubarb:
- In a medium saucepan, combine the diced rhubarb, granulated sugar, orange zest, orange juice, vanilla extract (if using), ground cinnamon or cardamom (if using), and water.
- Stir to combine all ingredients.

Simmer the Mixture:
- Place the saucepan over medium heat and bring the mixture to a gentle simmer, stirring occasionally.

Cook Until Softened:
- Reduce the heat to low and let the rhubarb cook gently for about 10-15 minutes, or until the rhubarb is soft and begins to break down, stirring occasionally.

Adjust Sweetness and Flavor:
- Taste the rhubarb sauce and adjust the sweetness by adding more sugar if desired.
- If you prefer a smoother sauce, you can use an immersion blender or transfer the mixture to a blender and blend until smooth.

Cool and Serve:
- Remove the saucepan from the heat and let the rhubarb sauce cool slightly.
- Serve the rhubarb sauce warm or chill it in the refrigerator before serving.

Storage:
- Store any leftover rhubarb sauce in a sealed container in the refrigerator for up to a week.

Serving Suggestions:

- Serve warm rhubarb sauce over vanilla ice cream or Greek yogurt.
- Use rhubarb sauce as a topping for pancakes, waffles, French toast, or oatmeal.
- Enjoy rhubarb sauce alongside roasted meats such as pork or chicken.
- Use rhubarb sauce as a filling for tarts, pies, or pastries.
- Stir rhubarb sauce into yogurt or smoothies for added flavor.

This homemade rhubarb sauce is a delicious way to enjoy the unique flavor of rhubarb. Feel free to adjust the sweetness and spices according to your taste preferences. Use this versatile sauce to enhance both sweet and savory dishes and enjoy the wonderful flavors of fresh rhubarb!

**Rhubarb Ice Cream**

Ingredients:

- 2 cups diced rhubarb (about 1/2-inch pieces)
- 1 cup granulated sugar
- 1 cup heavy cream
- 1 cup whole milk
- 4 large egg yolks
- 1 teaspoon vanilla extract
- Pinch of salt

Instructions:

Prepare the Rhubarb Compote:
- In a saucepan, combine the diced rhubarb and granulated sugar.
- Cook over medium heat, stirring occasionally, until the rhubarb is soft and breaks down into a compote-like consistency. This will take about 10-15 minutes.
- Remove from heat and let the rhubarb compote cool completely.

Prepare the Ice Cream Base:
- In a separate saucepan, combine the heavy cream and whole milk. Heat the mixture over medium heat until it just begins to simmer. Do not boil.
- In a bowl, whisk together the egg yolks until smooth.
- Gradually pour the hot cream mixture into the egg yolks, whisking constantly to temper the eggs.

Combine and Cook the Custard:
- Pour the egg mixture back into the saucepan.
- Cook over medium-low heat, stirring constantly with a wooden spoon or spatula, until the mixture thickens enough to coat the back of the spoon. This is called "coating the spoon" or until it reaches about 170°F (77°C) on a thermometer.
- Remove from heat and strain the custard through a fine-mesh sieve into a clean bowl to remove any cooked egg bits.

Cool and Chill:
- Stir the vanilla extract and a pinch of salt into the custard.
- Cover the bowl with plastic wrap, pressing it directly onto the surface of the custard to prevent a skin from forming.
- Chill the custard in the refrigerator until completely cold, preferably overnight.

Churn the Ice Cream:
- Once the rhubarb compote and custard are completely chilled, stir the rhubarb compote into the custard.
- Pour the mixture into an ice cream maker and churn according to the manufacturer's instructions until it reaches a soft-serve consistency.

Freeze and Serve:
- Transfer the churned ice cream into a freezer-safe container.
- Freeze for at least 4 hours or until firm.

Enjoy:
- Scoop the rhubarb ice cream into bowls or cones and enjoy!
- Garnish with additional rhubarb compote or fresh rhubarb slices if desired.

This homemade rhubarb ice cream is creamy, tangy, and utterly delicious. It's a perfect dessert for rhubarb lovers and a refreshing treat for warm days. Experiment with the sweetness level by adjusting the amount of sugar in the rhubarb compote and custard base to suit your taste preferences.

**Rhubarb Tart**

Ingredients:

For the Tart Crust:

- 1 1/2 cups all-purpose flour
- 1/2 cup powdered sugar
- 1/4 teaspoon salt
- 1/2 cup unsalted butter, cold and cut into small pieces
- 1 large egg yolk
- 1-2 tablespoons cold water, if needed

For the Rhubarb Filling:

- 4 cups sliced rhubarb (about 1/2-inch thick slices)
- 3/4 cup granulated sugar
- 2 tablespoons cornstarch
- 1/2 teaspoon vanilla extract

Instructions:

Prepare the Tart Crust:
- In a food processor, combine the flour, powdered sugar, and salt. Pulse to mix.
- Add the cold butter pieces and pulse until the mixture resembles coarse crumbs.
- Add the egg yolk and pulse again until the dough starts to come together. If needed, add cold water, 1 tablespoon at a time, until the dough forms a ball.
- Flatten the dough into a disk, wrap in plastic wrap, and refrigerate for at least 30 minutes.

Preheat the Oven:
- Preheat your oven to 375°F (190°C).

Roll Out the Dough:
- On a lightly floured surface, roll out the chilled dough into a circle about 12 inches in diameter.

- Transfer the rolled-out dough to a 9-inch tart pan with a removable bottom. Press the dough into the bottom and sides of the pan. Trim any excess dough hanging over the edges.

Prepare the Rhubarb Filling:
- In a large bowl, combine the sliced rhubarb, granulated sugar, cornstarch, and vanilla extract. Toss until the rhubarb is evenly coated.

Assemble the Tart:
- Arrange the rhubarb slices in an even layer inside the tart crust, filling the pan.

Bake the Tart:
- Place the tart pan on a baking sheet (to catch any drips) and bake in the preheated oven for 40-45 minutes, or until the rhubarb is tender and the crust is golden brown.

Cool and Serve:
- Allow the rhubarb tart to cool in the pan for about 10-15 minutes.
- Carefully remove the tart from the pan by gently pushing up the removable bottom.
- Let the tart cool completely on a wire rack before slicing and serving.

Optional Garnish:
- Serve the rhubarb tart as is, or with a dollop of whipped cream or vanilla ice cream for extra indulgence.

This rhubarb tart is a delightful dessert that showcases the natural tangy sweetness of rhubarb. Enjoy the tart on its own or with a scoop of vanilla ice cream for a perfect spring or summer treat! Feel free to adjust the sweetness of the filling according to your taste preference.

**Rhubarb Scones**

Ingredients:

- 2 cups all-purpose flour
- 1/4 cup granulated sugar
- 1 tablespoon baking powder
- 1/2 teaspoon salt
- 1/2 cup cold unsalted butter, cut into small cubes
- 1 cup diced rhubarb (about 1/2-inch pieces)
- 1/2 cup buttermilk
- 1 large egg
- 1 teaspoon vanilla extract
- Optional: Turbinado sugar, for sprinkling on top

Instructions:

Preheat the Oven and Prepare Baking Sheet:
- Preheat your oven to 400°F (200°C).
- Line a baking sheet with parchment paper or lightly grease it.

Prepare the Dry Ingredients:
- In a large mixing bowl, whisk together the flour, sugar, baking powder, and salt.

Cut in Butter:
- Add the cold cubed butter to the dry ingredients.
- Use a pastry cutter or two knives to cut the butter into the flour mixture until it resembles coarse crumbs. Some larger pea-sized pieces of butter are okay.

Add Rhubarb:
- Gently fold the diced rhubarb into the flour-butter mixture.

Combine Wet Ingredients:
- In a separate bowl, whisk together the buttermilk, egg, and vanilla extract.

Make Dough:
- Pour the wet ingredients into the dry ingredients.
- Use a fork or spatula to gently mix until the dough comes together. Be careful not to overmix.

Shape Scones:
- Transfer the dough onto a lightly floured surface.
- Pat the dough into a circle about 1-inch thick.
- Use a sharp knife to cut the dough into 8 wedges.

Bake the Scones:
- Place the scones on the prepared baking sheet, leaving some space between each.
- Optional: Brush the tops of the scones with a little buttermilk and sprinkle with turbinado sugar for a sweet crunch.

Bake and Serve:
- Bake the scones in the preheated oven for 18-20 minutes, or until golden brown on top and cooked through.

Cool and Enjoy:
- Remove the scones from the oven and let them cool on a wire rack.
- Serve the rhubarb scones warm or at room temperature with butter, jam, or clotted cream.

These rhubarb scones are perfect for breakfast, brunch, or afternoon tea. The rhubarb adds a delightful tartness to the scones, complementing the buttery and flaky texture. Enjoy these scones fresh from the oven for a delicious homemade treat! Feel free to adjust the sweetness by adding more or less sugar based on your preference.

**Rhubarb Jelly**

Ingredients:

- 4 cups chopped rhubarb (about 1/2-inch pieces)
- 4 cups granulated sugar
- 1 package (1.75 oz) powdered fruit pectin
- 1 lemon, juiced
- 4 cups water

Instructions:

Prepare the Rhubarb:
- Wash the rhubarb stalks and chop them into small pieces (about 1/2 inch).

Cook the Rhubarb:
- In a large saucepan, combine the chopped rhubarb and water.
- Bring the mixture to a boil over medium-high heat.
- Reduce the heat to low and simmer, uncovered, for about 10-15 minutes or until the rhubarb is soft and begins to break down.

Strain the Rhubarb Juice:
- Line a fine-mesh sieve or cheesecloth over a large bowl.
- Pour the cooked rhubarb mixture into the sieve to strain out the juice. Press down gently to extract as much juice as possible.
- Discard the solids (or save them for another use, like rhubarb sauce).

Make the Jelly:
- Measure 4 cups of the strained rhubarb juice into a clean saucepan.
- Add the lemon juice and powdered fruit pectin to the rhubarb juice. Stir well to combine.

Bring to a Boil:
- Place the saucepan over high heat and bring the rhubarb juice mixture to a full rolling boil, stirring constantly.

Add Sugar:
- Quickly stir in the granulated sugar all at once.
- Return the mixture to a full rolling boil and boil for exactly 1 minute, stirring constantly.

Skim Foam (if necessary):
- Remove the saucepan from the heat.
- Skim off any foam from the surface of the jelly with a metal spoon.

Fill Jars:

- Ladle the hot rhubarb jelly into sterilized jars, leaving about 1/4-inch headspace.
- Wipe the jar rims with a clean, damp cloth to remove any spills or residue.

Seal and Process (optional):

- Place sterilized lids on the jars and screw on the bands until fingertip tight.
- If you plan to store the jelly long-term, process the jars in a boiling water bath for 10 minutes (adjust time for altitude if needed).

Cool and Store:

- Allow the jars to cool completely at room temperature.
- Check the seals (the lids should not flex when pressed).
- Label the jars with the date and store them in a cool, dark place. Properly sealed jars can be stored for up to a year.

Serving Suggestions:

- Enjoy rhubarb jelly spread on toast, biscuits, scones, or crackers.
- Use rhubarb jelly as a topping for cheesecake, yogurt, or ice cream.
- Incorporate rhubarb jelly into recipes for glazes, sauces, or marinades.

This homemade rhubarb jelly captures the fresh flavor of rhubarb and is a delightful addition to your pantry. Adjust the sweetness by adding more or less sugar according to your taste preference. Enjoy this tangy and sweet jelly throughout the year!

**Rhubarb Punch**

Ingredients:

- 4 cups diced rhubarb
- 1 cup granulated sugar (adjust to taste)
- 4 cups water
- 1 lemon, sliced
- 1 orange, sliced
- 2 cups pineapple juice (or orange juice)
- 2 cups ginger ale or lemon-lime soda
- Ice cubes
- Fresh mint leaves, for garnish (optional)

Instructions:

Prepare the Rhubarb Syrup:
- In a large saucepan, combine the diced rhubarb, granulated sugar, and water.
- Bring the mixture to a boil over medium-high heat, then reduce the heat to low.
- Simmer the mixture for about 15-20 minutes, or until the rhubarb is soft and the liquid is slightly thickened.
- Remove the saucepan from heat and let the rhubarb mixture cool.

Strain the Rhubarb Syrup:
- Once the rhubarb mixture has cooled, strain it through a fine-mesh sieve or cheesecloth into a large pitcher or bowl. Press down on the solids to extract all the syrup.
- Discard the solids (or save them for another use, like rhubarb sauce).

Assemble the Punch:
- Add the sliced lemon and orange to the pitcher with the rhubarb syrup.
- Stir in the pineapple juice (or orange juice) to the mixture.

Chill the Punch:
- Place the pitcher in the refrigerator to chill the punch for at least 1 hour, allowing the flavors to meld.

Serve the Punch:
- Just before serving, add the ginger ale or lemon-lime soda to the chilled punch.
- Stir gently to combine.

Serve with Ice and Garnish:

- Fill glasses with ice cubes.
- Pour the rhubarb punch into the glasses.
- Garnish each glass with a fresh mint leaf, if desired.

Enjoy:
- Serve and enjoy this refreshing rhubarb punch with friends and family!

This rhubarb punch is a delightful and unique beverage that showcases the tart flavor of rhubarb combined with the sweetness of citrus and pineapple. Feel free to adjust the sweetness and tartness of the punch by adding more or less sugar or adjusting the amount of citrus juice. You can also customize this punch by adding other fruits or flavors to suit your taste preferences. Cheers to a delicious rhubarb-inspired drink!

**Rhubarb Cookies**

Ingredients:

- 1 cup diced rhubarb (about 1/2-inch pieces)
- 1/2 cup unsalted butter, softened
- 3/4 cup brown sugar
- 1/4 cup granulated sugar
- 1 large egg
- 1 teaspoon vanilla extract
- 1 1/2 cups all-purpose flour
- 1/2 teaspoon baking soda
- 1/4 teaspoon salt
- 1/2 cup chopped walnuts or pecans (optional)
- Optional: Powdered sugar, for dusting

Instructions:

Preheat the Oven:
- Preheat your oven to 350°F (175°C).
- Line baking sheets with parchment paper or silicone baking mats.

Prepare the Rhubarb:
- Wash the rhubarb stalks and dice them into small pieces (about 1/2 inch).

Cream Butter and Sugars:
- In a mixing bowl, cream together the softened butter, brown sugar, and granulated sugar until light and fluffy.

Add Egg and Vanilla:
- Beat in the egg and vanilla extract until well combined.

Mix Dry Ingredients:
- In a separate bowl, whisk together the flour, baking soda, and salt.

Combine Wet and Dry Ingredients:
- Gradually add the dry ingredients to the wet ingredients, mixing until just combined.
- Fold in the diced rhubarb and chopped nuts (if using).

Drop Cookies onto Baking Sheets:
- Drop tablespoonfuls of cookie dough onto the prepared baking sheets, spacing them about 2 inches apart.

Bake the Cookies:
- Bake in the preheated oven for 12-15 minutes, or until the edges are golden brown and the centers are set.

- Remove from the oven and let the cookies cool on the baking sheets for a few minutes before transferring them to wire racks to cool completely.

Optional Dusting:
- Once cooled, dust the tops of the cookies with powdered sugar for a decorative finish.

Enjoy:
- Serve and enjoy these soft and flavorful rhubarb cookies with a glass of milk or your favorite hot beverage.

These rhubarb cookies are a delightful treat that's perfect for showcasing the seasonal flavor of rhubarb. The combination of sweet cookie dough with tangy rhubarb pieces creates a unique and delicious cookie that's sure to be a hit with family and friends. Feel free to adjust the sweetness or add more nuts for extra texture. Store any leftover cookies in an airtight container for several days. Enjoy the wonderful flavors of rhubarb in this delightful cookie recipe!

**Rhubarb Crumble**

Ingredients:

For the Rhubarb Filling:

- 4 cups diced rhubarb (about 1/2-inch pieces)
- 1/2 cup granulated sugar (adjust based on the tartness of the rhubarb)
- 1 tablespoon all-purpose flour
- 1 teaspoon vanilla extract
- Zest of 1 orange (optional)

For the Crumble Topping:

- 1 cup old-fashioned rolled oats
- 3/4 cup all-purpose flour
- 1/2 cup packed brown sugar
- 1/2 teaspoon ground cinnamon
- 1/4 teaspoon salt
- 1/2 cup unsalted butter, melted

Instructions:

Preheat the Oven:
- Preheat your oven to 375°F (190°C). Grease a 9x9-inch (or similar size) baking dish with butter or cooking spray.

Prepare the Rhubarb Filling:
- In a large bowl, combine the diced rhubarb, granulated sugar, all-purpose flour, vanilla extract, and orange zest (if using). Toss until the rhubarb is evenly coated.

Make the Crumble Topping:
- In another bowl, mix together the rolled oats, all-purpose flour, brown sugar, ground cinnamon, and salt.
- Pour the melted butter over the oat mixture and stir until well combined and crumbly. The mixture should clump together when pressed.

Assemble the Crumble:
- Transfer the rhubarb filling into the greased baking dish, spreading it out evenly.

Add the Crumble Topping:

- Sprinkle the crumble topping evenly over the rhubarb filling, covering it completely.

Bake the Crumble:
- Place the baking dish in the preheated oven and bake for 35-40 minutes, or until the rhubarb is bubbling and the topping is golden brown and crisp.

Cool and Serve:
- Remove the rhubarb crumble from the oven and let it cool for a few minutes.
- Serve warm with a scoop of vanilla ice cream or a dollop of whipped cream.

Enjoy:
- Serve and enjoy this delicious rhubarb crumble as a comforting dessert!

This rhubarb crumble is best enjoyed warm, straight from the oven. The tangy rhubarb filling pairs perfectly with the sweet and crunchy oat topping. Feel free to customize this recipe by adding chopped nuts to the crumble topping or adjusting the sweetness of the filling according to your taste preferences. It's a delightful way to savor the flavors of rhubarb during its peak season!

**Rhubarb Pancakes**

Ingredients:

- 1 cup diced rhubarb
- 2 tablespoons granulated sugar
- 1 1/2 cups all-purpose flour
- 2 tablespoons granulated sugar
- 1 teaspoon baking powder
- 1/2 teaspoon baking soda
- 1/4 teaspoon salt
- 1 cup buttermilk (or substitute with 1 cup milk + 1 tablespoon lemon juice or vinegar)
- 1/4 cup unsalted butter, melted
- 1 large egg
- 1 teaspoon vanilla extract
- Butter or oil for cooking

Instructions:

Prepare the Rhubarb:
- In a small bowl, toss the diced rhubarb with 2 tablespoons of granulated sugar. Set aside and let it macerate while you prepare the pancake batter.

Prepare the Pancake Batter:
- In a large mixing bowl, whisk together the flour, 2 tablespoons of granulated sugar, baking powder, baking soda, and salt.

Combine Wet Ingredients:
- In another bowl, whisk together the buttermilk, melted butter, egg, and vanilla extract.

Make the Pancake Batter:
- Pour the wet ingredients into the dry ingredients and mix until just combined. Do not overmix; a few lumps in the batter are okay.

Fold in the Rhubarb:
- Gently fold the macerated rhubarb (along with any released juices) into the pancake batter.

Cook the Pancakes:
- Heat a griddle or non-stick skillet over medium heat. Add a small amount of butter or oil to coat the surface.
- Pour about 1/4 cup of pancake batter onto the griddle for each pancake, spacing them apart.

- Cook until bubbles form on the surface of the pancakes and the edges look set, about 2-3 minutes.

Flip and Cook the Other Side:
- Carefully flip the pancakes and cook for another 1-2 minutes, or until golden brown and cooked through.

Serve and Enjoy:
- Serve the rhubarb pancakes warm with butter, maple syrup, whipped cream, or additional diced rhubarb on top.

Optional Garnishes:
- Garnish with powdered sugar, sliced strawberries, or a dollop of Greek yogurt for extra flavor.

Repeat and Enjoy:
- Continue cooking the remaining batter in batches until all the pancakes are cooked.
- Serve immediately and enjoy these delicious rhubarb pancakes for breakfast or brunch!

These rhubarb pancakes are fluffy, flavorful, and perfect for celebrating the rhubarb season. The diced rhubarb adds a delightful tanginess to the pancakes, complementing the sweetness of the batter. Feel free to adjust the amount of sugar based on your preference for sweetness. Enjoy these pancakes with your favorite toppings for a wonderful morning treat!

**Rhubarb Upside-Down Cake**

Ingredients:

For the Rhubarb Topping:

- 4 cups sliced rhubarb (about 1/2-inch thick slices)
- 1 cup granulated sugar
- 1/4 cup unsalted butter

For the Cake Batter:

- 1 1/2 cups all-purpose flour
- 1 1/2 teaspoons baking powder
- 1/2 teaspoon baking soda
- 1/4 teaspoon salt
- 1/2 cup unsalted butter, softened
- 1 cup granulated sugar
- 2 large eggs
- 1 teaspoon vanilla extract
- 1 cup buttermilk

Instructions:

Preheat the Oven:
- Preheat your oven to 350°F (175°C).
- Grease a 9-inch round cake pan with butter or non-stick cooking spray.

Prepare the Rhubarb Topping:
- In a saucepan, combine the sliced rhubarb, granulated sugar, and 1/4 cup of unsalted butter.
- Cook over medium heat, stirring occasionally, until the rhubarb is tender and the sugar has dissolved, and the mixture is slightly caramelized. This will take about 8-10 minutes.
- Pour the rhubarb mixture into the prepared cake pan, spreading it out evenly on the bottom.

Make the Cake Batter:
- In a bowl, whisk together the flour, baking powder, baking soda, and salt.
- In a separate large mixing bowl, cream together the softened butter and granulated sugar until light and fluffy.

- Add the eggs, one at a time, beating well after each addition.
- Stir in the vanilla extract.
- Gradually add the flour mixture to the creamed butter mixture alternately with the buttermilk, beginning and ending with the flour mixture. Mix until just combined.

Assemble the Cake:
- Carefully pour the cake batter over the rhubarb mixture in the cake pan, spreading it out evenly.

Bake the Cake:
- Place the cake pan in the preheated oven and bake for 40-45 minutes, or until a toothpick inserted into the center of the cake comes out clean.

Cool and Invert the Cake:
- Remove the cake from the oven and let it cool in the pan for about 10 minutes.
- Run a knife around the edges of the cake to loosen it from the pan.
- Place a serving plate upside-down over the cake pan, then carefully invert the cake onto the plate. Tap the bottom of the cake pan to release the cake if needed.

Serve and Enjoy:
- Allow the rhubarb upside-down cake to cool slightly before slicing and serving.
- Serve slices of the cake warm or at room temperature, with whipped cream or vanilla ice cream if desired.

This rhubarb upside-down cake is a wonderful way to showcase the tart and sweet flavors of rhubarb in a beautiful and delicious dessert. The caramelized rhubarb topping adds a lovely touch to the moist and flavorful cake. Enjoy this cake with friends and family for a delightful treat!

**Rhubarb Vinaigrette**

Ingredients:

- 1 cup chopped rhubarb
- 1/4 cup water
- 1/4 cup white wine vinegar (or apple cider vinegar)
- 2 tablespoons honey (or maple syrup for vegan option)
- 1/4 cup extra virgin olive oil
- Salt and pepper, to taste

Instructions:

Cook the Rhubarb:
- In a small saucepan, combine the chopped rhubarb and water.
- Bring to a simmer over medium heat and cook until the rhubarb is very soft and tender, about 5-7 minutes.
- Remove from heat and let it cool slightly.

Blend the Vinaigrette:
- Transfer the cooked rhubarb to a blender or food processor.
- Add the white wine vinegar and honey (or maple syrup).
- Blend until smooth.

Emulsify with Olive Oil:
- With the blender running, slowly drizzle in the extra virgin olive oil until the vinaigrette is well combined and emulsified.
- Season with salt and pepper to taste.

Adjust Consistency (if needed):
- If the vinaigrette is too thick, you can thin it out with a little water or more vinegar until desired consistency is reached.

Serve and Enjoy:
- Use the rhubarb vinaigrette immediately or store it in an airtight container in the refrigerator for up to a week.
- Shake or stir well before using.

Serving Suggestions:

- Drizzle the rhubarb vinaigrette over mixed green salads, spinach salads, or grain salads.
- Use the vinaigrette as a marinade for grilled vegetables, chicken, or fish.
- Toss roasted vegetables with the vinaigrette before serving.

- Serve the vinaigrette as a dipping sauce for bread or crudité.

This rhubarb vinaigrette is a wonderful way to incorporate the tart and tangy flavor of rhubarb into your meals. It's versatile and can be used in various ways to enhance the flavors of salads and other dishes. Experiment with the sweetness level by adjusting the amount of honey or maple syrup according to your taste preferences. Enjoy this homemade rhubarb vinaigrette for a delicious and unique culinary experience!

## Rhubarb Margarita

Ingredients:

- 1 cup chopped rhubarb
- 1/2 cup water
- 1/4 cup granulated sugar
- 2 ounces silver tequila
- 1 ounce orange liqueur (e.g., Cointreau or triple sec)
- 1 ounce fresh lime juice
- Ice
- Salt or sugar (for rimming glasses, optional)
- Lime wedges, for garnish
- Rhubarb stalks, for garnish (optional)

Instructions:

Prepare the Rhubarb Syrup:
- In a small saucepan, combine the chopped rhubarb, water, and granulated sugar.
- Bring to a simmer over medium heat, stirring occasionally.
- Cook until the rhubarb is very soft and the sugar has dissolved, about 8-10 minutes.
- Remove from heat and let the mixture cool slightly.

Strain the Rhubarb Syrup:
- Strain the cooked rhubarb mixture through a fine-mesh sieve or cheesecloth into a bowl, pressing down on the solids to extract all the syrup. Discard the solids.

Prepare the Margarita:
- Rim the edges of your glasses with salt or sugar, if desired. To do this, rub a lime wedge around the rim of each glass and dip it into a shallow dish of salt or sugar.
- Fill the glasses with ice cubes.

Mix the Margarita:
- In a cocktail shaker filled with ice, combine 2 ounces of silver tequila, 1 ounce of orange liqueur, 1 ounce of fresh lime juice, and 1 ounce of the rhubarb syrup.
- Shake vigorously until well chilled.

Strain and Serve:
- Strain the margarita mixture into the prepared glasses over the ice.

Garnish and Enjoy:
- Garnish each glass with a lime wedge and a stalk of rhubarb, if desired.
- Serve immediately and enjoy your delicious rhubarb margarita!

Tips:

- Adjust the sweetness of the rhubarb syrup by adding more or less sugar according to your taste preferences.
- Feel free to experiment with different garnishes, such as fresh mint leaves or sliced jalapeños for a spicy kick.
- For a frozen rhubarb margarita, blend the margarita mixture with ice in a blender until smooth.

This rhubarb margarita is a delightful cocktail that's perfect for spring and summer gatherings. The tartness of the rhubarb syrup complements the citrusy and boozy flavors of the classic margarita, creating a refreshing and unique drink. Enjoy sipping this rhubarb-infused cocktail with friends and family!

**Rhubarb BBQ Sauce**

Ingredients:

- 2 cups chopped rhubarb (about 1/2-inch pieces)
- 1 cup chopped onion
- 2 cloves garlic, minced
- 1 cup ketchup
- 1/2 cup brown sugar
- 1/4 cup apple cider vinegar
- 2 tablespoons Worcestershire sauce
- 1 tablespoon Dijon mustard
- 1 teaspoon smoked paprika
- 1/2 teaspoon chili powder
- Salt and pepper, to taste
- 1 tablespoon olive oil

Instructions:

Prepare the Rhubarb:
- In a saucepan, heat olive oil over medium heat.
- Add the chopped onion and garlic to the pan. Sauté until the onions are translucent and fragrant, about 3-4 minutes.

Cook the Rhubarb:
- Add the chopped rhubarb to the saucepan with the onions and garlic.
- Cook for about 5-7 minutes, stirring occasionally, until the rhubarb is softened.

Add Remaining Ingredients:
- Stir in the ketchup, brown sugar, apple cider vinegar, Worcestershire sauce, Dijon mustard, smoked paprika, and chili powder.
- Season with salt and pepper to taste.

Simmer the Sauce:
- Bring the mixture to a simmer over medium-low heat.
- Reduce the heat to low and let the sauce simmer gently for about 20-25 minutes, stirring occasionally, until it thickens and the flavors meld together.

Blend (Optional):
- For a smooth consistency, you can blend the sauce using an immersion blender or transfer it to a regular blender. Be careful when blending hot liquids.

Adjust Consistency:
- If the sauce is too thick, you can add a little water or apple cider vinegar to reach your desired consistency.

Taste and Adjust Seasonings:
- Taste the BBQ sauce and adjust the seasoning to your liking. Add more brown sugar for sweetness, more vinegar for tanginess, or more chili powder for heat.

Cool and Store:
- Let the rhubarb BBQ sauce cool completely before transferring it to a jar or airtight container.
- Store the BBQ sauce in the refrigerator for up to 1-2 weeks.

Serving Suggestions:

- Use the rhubarb BBQ sauce as a glaze for grilled chicken, pork ribs, or tofu.
- Brush the sauce on vegetables before grilling or roasting.
- Serve the BBQ sauce alongside burgers, sandwiches, or as a dipping sauce for fries.

This homemade rhubarb BBQ sauce is flavorful, tangy, and perfect for adding a unique twist to your favorite BBQ dishes. Enjoy experimenting with this delicious sauce and incorporating the flavors of rhubarb into your cooking!

**Rhubarb Trifle**

Ingredients:

For the Rhubarb Compote:

- 4 cups chopped rhubarb
- 1 cup granulated sugar
- Zest and juice of 1 orange
- 1 teaspoon vanilla extract

For the Custard:

- 2 cups whole milk
- 1/2 cup granulated sugar
- 4 large egg yolks
- 1/4 cup cornstarch
- 1 teaspoon vanilla extract

For Assembling the Trifle:

- 1 prepared pound cake or sponge cake, sliced
- 2 cups heavy cream, whipped (sweetened with a bit of sugar, if desired)
- Fresh berries or mint leaves, for garnish (optional)

Instructions:

Make the Rhubarb Compote:
- In a saucepan, combine the chopped rhubarb, granulated sugar, orange zest, and orange juice.
- Cook over medium heat, stirring occasionally, until the rhubarb is soft and starts to break down, about 10-12 minutes.
- Remove from heat and stir in the vanilla extract. Let the compote cool completely.

Prepare the Custard:
- In a saucepan, heat the milk until steaming but not boiling.
- In a separate bowl, whisk together the sugar, egg yolks, and cornstarch until smooth.
- Gradually pour the hot milk into the egg mixture, whisking constantly.

- Return the mixture to the saucepan and cook over medium heat, stirring constantly, until the custard thickens and coats the back of a spoon.
- Remove from heat and stir in the vanilla extract.
- Transfer the custard to a bowl, cover with plastic wrap (directly touching the surface of the custard to prevent a skin from forming), and refrigerate until completely chilled.

Assemble the Trifle:
- Arrange slices of pound cake or sponge cake in the bottom of a trifle dish or a large glass bowl.
- Spoon half of the rhubarb compote over the cake layer.
- Pour half of the chilled custard over the rhubarb layer.
- Repeat with another layer of cake, followed by the remaining rhubarb compote and custard.

Finish with Whipped Cream:
- Top the trifle with a generous layer of whipped cream, spreading it out evenly.

Garnish and Chill:
- Garnish the trifle with fresh berries or mint leaves, if desired.
- Cover and refrigerate the trifle for at least 4 hours (or overnight) to allow the flavors to meld and the cake to absorb the juices.

Serve and Enjoy:
- Serve the rhubarb trifle chilled, scooping out portions to reveal the beautiful layers of cake, rhubarb compote, custard, and whipped cream.

This rhubarb trifle is a stunning dessert that's perfect for special occasions or casual gatherings. The combination of tangy rhubarb with creamy custard and fluffy cake is sure to impress your guests. Enjoy this delightful trifle as a refreshing and satisfying dessert!

**Rhubarb Syrup**

Ingredients:

- 4 cups chopped rhubarb (about 1/2-inch pieces)
- 2 cups granulated sugar
- 2 cups water
- Juice of 1 lemon (optional, for added tartness)

Instructions:

Prepare the Rhubarb:
- Wash the rhubarb stalks and chop them into small pieces (about 1/2 inch).

Cook the Rhubarb:
- In a saucepan, combine the chopped rhubarb, granulated sugar, and water.
- Optionally, add the juice of 1 lemon for additional tartness.
- Bring the mixture to a boil over medium-high heat, stirring occasionally.

Simmer and Infuse:
- Once boiling, reduce the heat to low and let the mixture simmer gently for about 15-20 minutes, or until the rhubarb is very soft and the liquid has thickened slightly.

Strain the Syrup:
- Remove the saucepan from the heat and let the mixture cool for a few minutes.
- Strain the rhubarb mixture through a fine-mesh sieve or cheesecloth into a bowl or pitcher. Press down on the solids to extract all the syrup.

Store the Syrup:
- Allow the rhubarb syrup to cool completely.
- Transfer the syrup into clean, sterilized bottles or jars with tight-fitting lids.

Enjoy the Rhubarb Syrup:
- Use the rhubarb syrup to flavor beverages like lemonade, cocktails, iced tea, or sparkling water.
- Drizzle the syrup over pancakes, waffles, or yogurt for a sweet and tangy topping.
- Incorporate the syrup into desserts, such as ice cream sundaes, cakes, or fruit salads.

Tips for Storing:

- Store the rhubarb syrup in the refrigerator for up to 2 weeks.
- For longer storage, you can freeze the syrup in ice cube trays and thaw as needed.
- Label and date the bottles or jars for easy identification.

This homemade rhubarb syrup is versatile and adds a delightful flavor to a variety of dishes and drinks. Experiment with different ways to use the syrup and enjoy the unique tartness of rhubarb in your favorite recipes!

**Rhubarb Smoothie**

Ingredients:

- 1 cup chopped rhubarb (fresh or frozen)
- 1 banana, fresh or frozen
- 1 cup mixed berries (such as strawberries, raspberries, or blueberries)
- 1 cup plain Greek yogurt (or dairy-free alternative)
- 1-2 tablespoons honey or maple syrup (adjust to taste)
- 1/2 - 1 cup unsweetened almond milk or other milk of choice
- Ice cubes (if using fresh fruit)

Instructions:

Prepare the Rhubarb:
- If using fresh rhubarb, wash and chop it into small pieces. If using frozen rhubarb, there's no need to thaw.

Cook the Rhubarb (Optional):
- In a small saucepan, combine the chopped rhubarb with a splash of water.
- Cook over medium heat until the rhubarb softens, about 5-7 minutes. This step is optional but helps to mellow the tartness of rhubarb.

Combine Ingredients:
- In a blender, combine the cooked (or raw) rhubarb, banana, mixed berries, Greek yogurt, honey or maple syrup, and almond milk.

Blend Until Smooth:
- Blend the ingredients until smooth and creamy. Add more almond milk as needed to reach your desired consistency. If using fresh fruit instead of frozen, you can add a handful of ice cubes to chill the smoothie.

Taste and Adjust:
- Taste the smoothie and adjust sweetness with more honey or maple syrup if desired.

Serve and Enjoy:
- Pour the rhubarb smoothie into glasses and serve immediately.
- Garnish with fresh berries or a slice of rhubarb for a decorative touch, if desired.

Tips:

- Feel free to customize the smoothie by adding other fruits like pineapple, mango, or peaches.

- For a creamier texture, you can substitute part of the Greek yogurt with coconut milk or avocado.
- If you prefer a thinner smoothie, add more almond milk or water.
- This smoothie can be made ahead of time and stored in the refrigerator for a few hours. Give it a quick stir before serving.

Enjoy this vibrant and flavorful rhubarb smoothie as a nutritious breakfast, snack, or post-workout refresher. It's a delightful way to incorporate the seasonal flavors of rhubarb into your daily routine!

**Rhubarb Popsicles**

Ingredients:

- 2 cups chopped rhubarb
- 1/2 cup granulated sugar (adjust to taste depending on the tartness of the rhubarb)
- 1 cup water
- 1 tablespoon freshly squeezed lemon juice
- Popsicle molds
- Popsicle sticks

Instructions:

Prepare the Rhubarb Mixture:
- In a saucepan, combine the chopped rhubarb, granulated sugar, and water.
- Bring the mixture to a boil over medium heat, then reduce the heat to low.
- Simmer the rhubarb mixture for about 10-12 minutes, or until the rhubarb is very soft and starts to break down.

Blend the Mixture:
- Remove the saucepan from the heat and let the rhubarb mixture cool slightly.
- Transfer the cooked rhubarb mixture to a blender or food processor.
- Add the freshly squeezed lemon juice.
- Blend until smooth and well combined.

Fill the Popsicle Molds:
- Pour the blended rhubarb mixture into popsicle molds, leaving a little space at the top for expansion.
- Insert popsicle sticks into the molds.

Freeze the Popsicles:
- Place the popsicle molds in the freezer and freeze for at least 4-6 hours, or until the popsicles are completely frozen.

Unmold and Enjoy:
- Once the rhubarb popsicles are frozen solid, remove the molds from the freezer.
- To release the popsicles, run the molds briefly under warm water to loosen the popsicles.
- Carefully remove the popsicles from the molds and enjoy immediately!

Tips:

- Feel free to adjust the sweetness of the rhubarb mixture by adding more or less sugar based on your preference.
- For added texture and flavor, you can stir in finely chopped fresh strawberries or raspberries into the rhubarb mixture before pouring into the molds.
- If you prefer a creamier popsicle, you can swirl in a bit of Greek yogurt or coconut milk into the rhubarb mixture before freezing.

These homemade rhubarb popsicles are a delicious and healthier alternative to store-bought popsicles, with the unique flavor of tart rhubarb shining through. They're perfect for kids and adults alike, and you can enjoy them as a cool treat on a warm summer day. Experiment with different variations and enjoy the refreshing taste of rhubarb in popsicle form!

**Rhubarb Cheesecake**

Ingredients:

For the Crust:

- 1 1/2 cups graham cracker crumbs
- 1/4 cup granulated sugar
- 6 tablespoons unsalted butter, melted

For the Rhubarb Compote:

- 4 cups chopped rhubarb
- 1 cup granulated sugar
- Zest and juice of 1 orange
- 1 teaspoon vanilla extract

For the Cheesecake Filling:

- 24 ounces (3 packages) cream cheese, softened
- 1 cup granulated sugar
- 3 large eggs
- 1 teaspoon vanilla extract
- 1/2 cup sour cream

Instructions:

1. Prepare the Rhubarb Compote:

- In a saucepan, combine the chopped rhubarb, granulated sugar, orange zest, and orange juice.
- Cook over medium heat, stirring occasionally, until the rhubarb is soft and starts to break down, about 10-12 minutes.
- Remove from heat and stir in the vanilla extract. Let the compote cool completely.

2. Make the Crust:

- Preheat your oven to 325°F (160°C).
- In a bowl, mix together the graham cracker crumbs, granulated sugar, and melted butter until well combined.
- Press the mixture into the bottom of a 9-inch springform pan to form an even crust.
- Bake the crust for 10 minutes, then remove from the oven and let it cool while you prepare the filling.

3. Prepare the Cheesecake Filling:

- In a large mixing bowl, beat the softened cream cheese and granulated sugar until smooth and creamy.
- Add the eggs one at a time, beating well after each addition.
- Stir in the vanilla extract and sour cream until smooth and well combined.

4. Assemble the Cheesecake:

- Spread half of the rhubarb compote over the cooled crust, reserving the other half for topping.
- Pour the cheesecake filling over the rhubarb layer in the springform pan, spreading it out evenly.

5. Bake the Cheesecake:

- Place the cheesecake in the preheated oven and bake for 45-50 minutes, or until the edges are set and the center is slightly jiggly.
- Turn off the oven and let the cheesecake cool in the oven with the door slightly open for 1 hour.

6. Chill and Serve:

- Remove the cheesecake from the oven and let it cool completely at room temperature.
- Once cooled, cover the cheesecake with plastic wrap and refrigerate for at least 4 hours or overnight to set.

7. Garnish and Serve:

- Before serving, spread the remaining rhubarb compote over the top of the chilled cheesecake.
- Carefully remove the sides of the springform pan.
- Slice the rhubarb cheesecake and serve chilled. Enjoy!

This rhubarb cheesecake is a perfect dessert for rhubarb lovers and cheesecake enthusiasts alike. The creamy texture of the cheesecake pairs beautifully with the tartness of the rhubarb compote, creating a delightful balance of flavors. Serve this delicious dessert at your next gathering and watch it disappear!

**Rhubarb Relish**

Ingredients:

- 4 cups chopped rhubarb
- 1 cup chopped red onion
- 1 cup diced red bell pepper
- 1 cup apple cider vinegar
- 1 cup packed brown sugar
- 1/2 cup golden raisins (optional)
- 1 tablespoon grated fresh ginger
- 1 teaspoon mustard seeds
- 1/2 teaspoon salt
- 1/2 teaspoon black pepper
- Pinch of red pepper flakes (optional, for heat)

Instructions:

Prepare the Ingredients:
- Wash and chop the rhubarb into small pieces.
- Chop the red onion and red bell pepper into small dice.
- Grate the fresh ginger.

Cook the Relish:
- In a large saucepan or pot, combine the chopped rhubarb, red onion, red bell pepper, apple cider vinegar, brown sugar, golden raisins (if using), grated ginger, mustard seeds, salt, black pepper, and red pepper flakes (if using).
- Stir to combine all the ingredients.

Simmer the Mixture:
- Bring the mixture to a boil over medium-high heat, stirring occasionally.
- Reduce the heat to low and let the relish simmer gently for about 30-40 minutes, or until it thickens and the rhubarb breaks down, stirring occasionally.

Adjust Seasoning:
- Taste the rhubarb relish and adjust the seasoning if needed. Add more sugar for sweetness or more vinegar for tartness, according to your preference.

Cool and Store:
- Remove the pot from the heat and let the rhubarb relish cool to room temperature.

- Transfer the relish to clean, sterilized jars with tight-fitting lids.

Store in the Refrigerator:
- Once cooled, seal the jars tightly and store the rhubarb relish in the refrigerator.
- The relish will continue to develop flavor over time and can be stored in the refrigerator for up to a few weeks.

Serving Suggestions:

- Serve the rhubarb relish as a condiment for grilled meats, such as chicken, pork, or lamb.
- Use the relish as a topping for burgers or sandwiches.
- Pair the relish with cheeses on a charcuterie board or cheese platter.
- Enjoy the relish as a side accompaniment to roasted vegetables or grilled fish.

This homemade rhubarb relish is a wonderful way to preserve the flavors of rhubarb and add a burst of tangy sweetness to your favorite dishes. It's a versatile condiment that's perfect for adding a unique twist to your meals. Experiment with different serving ideas and enjoy the delicious flavors of rhubarb relish!

**Rhubarb Compote**

Ingredients:

- 4 cups chopped rhubarb (about 1/2-inch pieces)
- 1 cup granulated sugar (adjust amount based on desired sweetness and tartness of rhubarb)
- Zest and juice of 1 orange (optional, for added flavor)
- 1 teaspoon vanilla extract (optional)

Instructions:

Prepare the Rhubarb:
- Wash the rhubarb stalks and trim off any leaves (which are not edible).
- Chop the rhubarb into small pieces, about 1/2-inch in size.

Cook the Rhubarb:
- In a saucepan, combine the chopped rhubarb, granulated sugar, and optional orange zest and juice.
- Place the saucepan over medium heat and stir gently to combine the ingredients.

Simmer the Mixture:
- Bring the rhubarb mixture to a gentle simmer, stirring occasionally to dissolve the sugar.
- Reduce the heat to low and let the mixture cook for about 10-12 minutes, or until the rhubarb pieces are tender and begin to break down. Stir occasionally to prevent sticking.

Add Vanilla (Optional):
- Remove the saucepan from heat.
- Stir in the vanilla extract, if using, to add a hint of flavor.

Cool and Serve:
- Allow the rhubarb compote to cool slightly before serving.
- Transfer the compote to a bowl or jar for storage.

Store the Compote:
- Once cooled, store the rhubarb compote in the refrigerator.
- It can be kept in an airtight container for up to a week.

Serving Suggestions:

- Serve the rhubarb compote warm or chilled.
- Enjoy it as a topping for yogurt, oatmeal, pancakes, waffles, or French toast.

- Use the compote as a filling for pies, tarts, or cakes.
- Swirl the compote into vanilla ice cream or use it to make rhubarb sundaes.
- Add a spoonful of rhubarb compote to cocktails or mocktails for a tangy twist.

Rhubarb compote is a delightful way to enjoy the unique flavor of rhubarb. Adjust the sweetness and additional flavors (like orange zest or vanilla) according to your taste preferences. This versatile compote can be used in various ways to enhance both sweet and savory dishes. Enjoy experimenting with this delicious rhubarb preparation!

**Rhubarb Slush**

Ingredients:

For the Rhubarb Syrup:

- 4 cups chopped rhubarb
- 2 cups granulated sugar
- 2 cups water
- Juice of 1 lemon
- Zest of 1 lemon (optional)

For the Rhubarb Slush:

- Rhubarb syrup (from the recipe above)
- Ice cubes
- Sparkling water or soda (for a non-alcoholic version)
- Vodka or gin (optional, for a spiked version)
- Fresh mint leaves or lemon slices, for garnish

Instructions:

1. Prepare the Rhubarb Syrup:

- In a saucepan, combine the chopped rhubarb, granulated sugar, water, lemon juice, and lemon zest (if using).
- Bring the mixture to a boil over medium-high heat, stirring occasionally.
- Reduce the heat to low and simmer for about 15-20 minutes, or until the rhubarb is soft and the liquid has thickened slightly.
- Remove from heat and let the syrup cool completely.
- Strain the syrup through a fine-mesh sieve or cheesecloth to remove any solids. Transfer the syrup to a jar or container and refrigerate until chilled.

2. Make the Rhubarb Slush:

- In a blender, combine the rhubarb syrup with ice cubes. Use about 1 part rhubarb syrup to 2 parts ice cubes, depending on your desired slushiness.
- Blend until the mixture is smooth and slushy.

3. Serve the Rhubarb Slush:

- Pour the rhubarb slush into glasses.
- For a non-alcoholic version, top off the slush with sparkling water or soda and stir gently.
- For a spiked version, add a shot of vodka or gin to each glass and stir to combine.
- Garnish with fresh mint leaves or lemon slices, if desired.

4. Enjoy!

- Serve the rhubarb slush immediately while cold and refreshing.
- Sip and enjoy this delightful and tangy summer drink!

Tips:

- Customize the sweetness of the rhubarb syrup by adjusting the amount of sugar based on your preference and the tartness of the rhubarb.
- Feel free to experiment with different herbs or spices in the syrup, such as ginger or cinnamon, for added flavor.
- Make a large batch of rhubarb syrup and store it in the refrigerator to enjoy rhubarb slush anytime.
- This recipe can be easily doubled or tripled for a crowd.

Rhubarb slush is a fantastic way to enjoy the unique flavor of rhubarb in a fun and refreshing drink. Whether you prefer a non-alcoholic version or want to add a splash of spirits, this rhubarb slush will be a hit at your next gathering or summer celebration. Cheers to cooling down with this delicious rhubarb treat!

**Rhubarb Wine**

Ingredients:

- 5-6 pounds of fresh rhubarb stalks
- 3 pounds of granulated sugar (adjust based on desired sweetness)
- 1 gallon of water (filtered or spring water is best)
- 1 packet of wine yeast (suitable for fruit wines)
- 1 teaspoon of yeast nutrient (optional, to aid fermentation)
- Campden tablets (potassium metabisulfite) or other sanitizer for sterilizing equipment

Equipment Needed:

- Large fermentation vessel (e.g., glass carboy or food-grade plastic bucket)
- Airlock and bung (or a balloon)
- Nylon straining bag or cheesecloth
- Funnel
- Hydrometer (for measuring specific gravity)
- Siphon tube
- Wine bottles and corks (or other suitable containers for bottling)

Instructions:

1. Prepare the Rhubarb:

- Wash the rhubarb stalks thoroughly and trim off the leaves (which are toxic and should not be used).
- Chop the rhubarb into small pieces (about 1-inch in size).

2. Make the Rhubarb Must:

- In a large pot, combine the chopped rhubarb with the water and bring to a boil.
- Reduce heat and simmer for about 20-30 minutes, or until the rhubarb breaks down and releases its juices.
- Remove from heat and let the rhubarb mixture cool to room temperature.

3. Strain the Rhubarb Juice:

- Place a nylon straining bag or cheesecloth over a fermentation vessel (e.g., a glass carboy or plastic bucket).
- Pour the cooled rhubarb mixture into the straining bag to filter out the solids, allowing the rhubarb juice to collect in the vessel.

4. Add Sugar and Yeast:

- Stir in the granulated sugar into the rhubarb juice until dissolved.
- Check the temperature of the rhubarb must (it should be around 70-75°F or 21-24°C).
- Sprinkle the wine yeast over the surface of the must and gently stir to combine.
- If using yeast nutrient, add it according to the manufacturer's instructions.

5. Fermentation:

- Fit the fermentation vessel with an airlock filled with sanitizer or use a balloon secured with a rubber band to allow gases to escape during fermentation.
- Place the vessel in a cool, dark area with a stable temperature (around 60-70°F or 15-21°C) and allow the rhubarb wine to ferment for about 1-2 weeks.
- Stir the must daily to aerate and promote yeast activity.

6. Rack the Wine:

- After primary fermentation slows down (bubbling subsides), siphon the wine into a clean fermentation vessel, leaving behind any sediment (lees) at the bottom.
- Fit the new vessel with an airlock and allow the wine to undergo secondary fermentation for another 4-6 weeks, or until fermentation completes.

7. Bottling:

- Once fermentation is complete (no more bubbles and wine clears), siphon the rhubarb wine into clean wine bottles.
- Cork the bottles securely and store them upright in a cool, dark place for aging.

8. Aging and Enjoying:

- Rhubarb wine benefits from aging for several months to develop its flavors.

- After aging, chill the wine before serving and enjoy the unique taste of homemade rhubarb wine!

Notes:

- Remember to sanitize all equipment thoroughly to prevent contamination and off-flavors in your wine.
- Adjust the sugar content based on your taste preferences and the natural sweetness of the rhubarb.
- Feel free to experiment with different yeast strains or additional flavorings (such as lemon zest or spices) to customize your rhubarb wine.

Making rhubarb wine is a rewarding process that allows you to savor the flavors of this unique ingredient in a delightful beverage. Enjoy your homemade rhubarb wine with friends and family, and cheers to your winemaking adventure!

**Rhubarb Glaze**

Ingredients:

- 2 cups chopped fresh rhubarb
- 1/2 cup water
- 1/2 cup sugar (adjust to taste depending on the tartness of the rhubarb)
- 1 tablespoon lemon juice
- 1 teaspoon cornstarch (optional, for thickening)

Instructions:

Prepare the Rhubarb:
- Rinse the rhubarb stalks thoroughly and trim off the ends. Cut the rhubarb into small pieces, about 1-inch in length.

Cook the Rhubarb:
- In a saucepan, combine the chopped rhubarb, water, sugar, and lemon juice.
- Cook over medium heat, stirring occasionally, until the rhubarb starts to break down and becomes soft. This will take about 10-15 minutes.

Thicken the Glaze (Optional):
- If you prefer a thicker glaze, mix the cornstarch with a tablespoon of water to create a slurry.
- Stir the cornstarch slurry into the simmering rhubarb mixture.
- Continue to cook for another 1-2 minutes until the glaze thickens slightly.

Strain (Optional):
- For a smoother glaze, you can strain the cooked rhubarb mixture through a fine-mesh sieve to remove any remaining fibrous bits.

Cool and Serve:
- Remove the saucepan from the heat and let the glaze cool slightly.
- Use the rhubarb glaze immediately as a topping for desserts like cheesecake, pound cake, or ice cream. Alternatively, store it in the refrigerator in an airtight container for up to a week.

Tips:

- Adjust the sweetness of the glaze by adding more or less sugar, depending on your taste preference and the tartness of the rhubarb.
- This glaze works wonderfully with both sweet and savory dishes. Experiment with using it as a sauce for roasted meats or grilled vegetables.

- Feel free to add complementary flavors such as vanilla extract or orange zest for added depth.

Enjoy your homemade rhubarb glaze!

**Rhubarb Shortcake**

Ingredients:

For the Rhubarb Filling:

- 4 cups chopped rhubarb (about 1/2-inch pieces)
- 1 cup granulated sugar
- 1 tablespoon cornstarch
- 1/4 cup water
- 1 teaspoon vanilla extract

For the Shortcake:

- 2 cups all-purpose flour
- 1/4 cup granulated sugar
- 1 tablespoon baking powder
- 1/2 teaspoon salt
- 1/2 cup cold unsalted butter, cubed
- 2/3 cup milk
- 1 teaspoon vanilla extract

For Serving:

- Whipped cream or vanilla ice cream (optional)

Instructions:

1. Prepare the Rhubarb Filling:

- In a saucepan, combine the chopped rhubarb, sugar, cornstarch, and water.
- Cook over medium heat, stirring occasionally, until the mixture starts to simmer and the rhubarb begins to soften.
- Reduce the heat to low and simmer gently for about 8-10 minutes or until the rhubarb is tender and the mixture has thickened slightly.
- Remove from heat and stir in the vanilla extract. Set aside to cool.

2. Make the Shortcake:

- Preheat your oven to 400°F (200°C). Line a baking sheet with parchment paper.
- In a large mixing bowl, whisk together the flour, sugar, baking powder, and salt.
- Cut in the cold butter using a pastry cutter or fork until the mixture resembles coarse crumbs.
- In a separate bowl, mix together the milk and vanilla extract.
- Gradually add the milk mixture to the flour mixture, stirring until a dough forms.
- Turn the dough out onto a lightly floured surface and gently knead a few times until it comes together.
- Roll out the dough to about 1/2-inch thickness. Use a biscuit cutter or a glass to cut out rounds of dough.
- Place the dough rounds onto the prepared baking sheet.
- Bake for 12-15 minutes or until the shortcakes are golden brown.

3. Assemble the Rhubarb Shortcake:

- Allow the shortcakes to cool slightly after baking.
- Slice each shortcake in half horizontally.
- Spoon a generous amount of the cooked rhubarb filling onto the bottom halves of the shortcakes.
- Replace the top halves of the shortcakes over the rhubarb filling.
- Serve warm, topped with whipped cream or vanilla ice cream if desired.

Enjoy your homemade rhubarb shortcake, a perfect blend of textures and flavors! This dessert is a delightful way to showcase the unique taste of rhubarb in a classic summer treat.

**Rhubarb Chiffon Pie**

Ingredients:

For the Crust:

- 1 1/2 cups graham cracker crumbs (or digestive biscuit crumbs)
- 6 tablespoons unsalted butter, melted
- 1/4 cup granulated sugar

For the Rhubarb Filling:

- 3 cups chopped rhubarb (about 1/2-inch pieces)
- 1 cup granulated sugar
- 1 envelope (2 1/4 teaspoons) unflavored gelatin
- 1/4 cup cold water
- 3 large egg yolks
- 1/2 cup water
- 1/4 teaspoon salt
- 1/2 cup heavy cream

For the Chiffon Topping:

- 3 large egg whites
- 1/4 cup granulated sugar
- 1/4 teaspoon cream of tartar
- 1 teaspoon vanilla extract

Instructions:

1. Prepare the Crust:

- Preheat your oven to 350°F (175°C).
- In a bowl, combine the graham cracker crumbs, melted butter, and sugar.
- Press the mixture firmly into the bottom and up the sides of a 9-inch pie dish.
- Bake the crust for 10 minutes, then remove from the oven and let it cool completely.

2. Make the Rhubarb Filling:

   - In a saucepan, combine the chopped rhubarb and sugar. Cook over medium heat until the rhubarb is tender, about 10-12 minutes.
   - In a small bowl, sprinkle the gelatin over 1/4 cup of cold water and let it soften for a few minutes.
   - In another bowl, whisk together the egg yolks, 1/2 cup water, and salt.
   - Gradually add the hot rhubarb mixture to the egg yolk mixture, whisking constantly.
   - Return the mixture to the saucepan and cook over low heat, stirring constantly, until slightly thickened.
   - Remove from heat and stir in the softened gelatin until dissolved.
   - Let the rhubarb filling cool to room temperature.

3. Prepare the Chiffon Topping:

   - In a heatproof bowl, combine the egg whites, sugar, and cream of tartar.
   - Place the bowl over a pot of simmering water (double boiler method) and whisk continuously until the sugar is dissolved and the mixture is warm to the touch.
   - Remove from heat and beat the egg white mixture using an electric mixer until stiff peaks form.
   - Gently fold in the vanilla extract.

4. Assemble the Pie:

   - In a separate bowl, whip the heavy cream until stiff peaks form.
   - Gently fold the whipped cream into the cooled rhubarb filling until well combined.
   - Spoon the rhubarb filling into the cooled pie crust.
   - Spread the chiffon topping over the rhubarb filling, creating decorative swirls with a spoon or spatula.
   - Refrigerate the pie for at least 4 hours or until set.

5. Serve and Enjoy:

   - Slice and serve the rhubarb chiffon pie chilled.
   - Optionally, garnish with additional whipped cream or fresh rhubarb slices before serving.

This rhubarb chiffon pie is a delightful and airy dessert that's perfect for showcasing the unique flavor of rhubarb. Enjoy!

**Rhubarb Breakfast Bars**

Ingredients:

For the Rhubarb Filling:

- 3 cups chopped rhubarb (about 1/2-inch pieces)
- 1/2 cup granulated sugar
- 2 tablespoons water
- 1 tablespoon cornstarch
- 1 teaspoon vanilla extract

For the Oat Crust and Topping:

- 1 1/2 cups old-fashioned rolled oats
- 1 1/2 cups all-purpose flour
- 1 cup packed brown sugar
- 1/2 teaspoon baking soda
- 1/4 teaspoon salt
- 1 cup unsalted butter, melted
- 1 teaspoon vanilla extract

Instructions:

1. Preheat the Oven:

- Preheat your oven to 350°F (175°C). Grease a 9x13-inch baking dish or line it with parchment paper.

2. Prepare the Rhubarb Filling:

- In a saucepan, combine the chopped rhubarb, granulated sugar, and water.
- Cook over medium heat until the rhubarb starts to break down and become tender, about 8-10 minutes.
- In a small bowl, mix the cornstarch with a tablespoon of water to create a slurry.
- Stir the cornstarch slurry into the rhubarb mixture and cook for another 1-2 minutes until thickened.
- Remove from heat and stir in the vanilla extract. Set aside to cool slightly.

3. Make the Oat Crust and Topping:

- In a large mixing bowl, combine the rolled oats, flour, brown sugar, baking soda, and salt.
- Add the melted butter and vanilla extract to the dry ingredients. Stir until well combined and crumbly.
- Reserve about 1 1/2 cups of the mixture for the topping. Press the remaining mixture evenly into the bottom of the prepared baking dish.

4. Assemble the Bars:

- Spread the rhubarb filling over the oat crust in the baking dish, making sure it's evenly distributed.
- Sprinkle the reserved oat mixture evenly over the rhubarb filling, creating a crumbly topping.

5. Bake and Serve:

- Bake the bars in the preheated oven for 30-35 minutes or until the top is golden brown.
- Remove from the oven and let the bars cool completely in the baking dish before cutting into squares.
- Serve the rhubarb breakfast bars at room temperature or slightly warmed.

6. Storage:

- Store any leftover bars in an airtight container at room temperature for up to 3 days, or refrigerate for longer shelf life.

These rhubarb breakfast bars are perfect for a quick and delicious morning treat or a delightful snack any time of day. Enjoy the combination of sweet, tart, and crumbly flavors in every bite!

**Rhubarb Daiquiri**

Ingredients:

- 2 oz white rum
- 1 oz fresh rhubarb syrup (see recipe below)
- 1 oz fresh lime juice
- Ice
- Rhubarb stalk or lime twist, for garnish

For the Rhubarb Syrup:

- 1 cup chopped rhubarb
- 1 cup granulated sugar
- 1 cup water

Instructions:

1. Make the Rhubarb Syrup:

- In a saucepan, combine the chopped rhubarb, sugar, and water.
- Bring the mixture to a boil over medium-high heat, stirring occasionally to dissolve the sugar.
- Reduce the heat to low and simmer for about 10-15 minutes, or until the rhubarb is soft and the mixture has thickened slightly.
- Remove from heat and let the syrup cool completely.
- Strain the syrup through a fine mesh sieve to remove the solids. Store the syrup in the refrigerator until ready to use.

2. Prepare the Rhubarb Daiquiri:

- In a cocktail shaker, combine the white rum, fresh rhubarb syrup, and fresh lime juice.
- Fill the shaker with ice.
- Shake vigorously until well chilled, about 15-20 seconds.
- Strain the mixture into a chilled cocktail glass.

3. Garnish and Serve:

- Garnish your Rhubarb Daiquiri with a rhubarb stalk or a twist of lime peel.
- Serve immediately and enjoy!

Tips:

- Adjust the sweetness of the cocktail by varying the amount of rhubarb syrup added to suit your taste.
- For a fun variation, try using aged rum instead of white rum for a more complex flavor profile.
- You can make a larger batch of rhubarb syrup and store it in the refrigerator for up to a week to use in multiple cocktails.

This Rhubarb Daiquiri is perfect for warm weather gatherings or simply for enjoying a taste of summer at home. The tartness of the rhubarb combined with the rum and lime creates a delightful and unique cocktail experience. Cheers!

**Rhubarb Salad Dressing**

Ingredients:

- 1 cup chopped rhubarb
- 1/4 cup water
- 2 tablespoons honey or maple syrup
- 2 tablespoons apple cider vinegar
- 1 tablespoon Dijon mustard
- Salt and pepper, to taste
- 1/4 cup olive oil or neutral-flavored oil (such as avocado oil)

Instructions:

1. Cook the Rhubarb:

- In a small saucepan, combine the chopped rhubarb and water.
- Cook over medium heat, stirring occasionally, until the rhubarb breaks down and becomes very soft, about 8-10 minutes.
- Remove from heat and let the cooked rhubarb mixture cool slightly.

2. Blend the Dressing:

- Transfer the cooked rhubarb mixture to a blender or food processor.
- Add honey (or maple syrup), apple cider vinegar, Dijon mustard, salt, and pepper.
- Blend until smooth and well combined.

3. Emulsify with Oil:

- With the blender or food processor running on low speed, slowly drizzle in the olive oil (or other neutral oil) until the dressing is emulsified and creamy.
- Continue blending until the oil is fully incorporated into the dressing.

4. Adjust Seasoning:

- Taste the dressing and adjust the seasoning, adding more salt, pepper, honey, or vinegar as needed to achieve the desired balance of flavors.

5. Serve:

- Use the rhubarb salad dressing immediately over your favorite salad greens or vegetables.
- Store any leftover dressing in a sealed container in the refrigerator for up to one week. Shake or stir well before using.

Tips:

- This rhubarb salad dressing pairs wonderfully with salads featuring fresh greens, strawberries, goat cheese, almonds, or grilled chicken.
- Feel free to adjust the sweetness of the dressing by adding more or less honey or maple syrup, depending on your preference.
- For a smoother dressing, strain the blended mixture through a fine mesh sieve to remove any fibrous bits of rhubarb before adding the oil.

Enjoy this unique and flavorful rhubarb salad dressing to elevate your salads with a delightful tangy twist!

**Rhubarb Marinade**

Ingredients:

- 1 cup chopped rhubarb
- 1/4 cup honey or maple syrup
- 1/4 cup soy sauce (or tamari for gluten-free option)
- 2 tablespoons apple cider vinegar
- 2 cloves garlic, minced
- 1 tablespoon grated fresh ginger (optional)
- 1/4 teaspoon black pepper
- 2 tablespoons olive oil or neutral-flavored oil (such as avocado oil)
- Salt, to taste

Instructions:

1. Prepare the Rhubarb:

- Rinse the rhubarb stalks thoroughly and trim off the ends. Chop the rhubarb into small pieces.

2. Cook the Rhubarb:

- In a small saucepan, combine the chopped rhubarb, honey (or maple syrup), soy sauce (or tamari), apple cider vinegar, minced garlic, grated ginger (if using), and black pepper.
- Cook over medium heat, stirring occasionally, until the rhubarb breaks down and becomes soft, about 8-10 minutes.
- Remove from heat and let the cooked rhubarb mixture cool slightly.

3. Blend the Marinade:

- Transfer the cooked rhubarb mixture to a blender or food processor.
- Blend until smooth and well combined.

4. Add Oil and Seasoning:

- With the blender or food processor running on low speed, slowly drizzle in the olive oil (or other neutral oil) until the marinade is emulsified and smooth.
- Taste the marinade and add salt as needed, depending on your preference.

5. Marinade Your Dish:

- Place your choice of protein (such as chicken, pork, tofu, or vegetables) in a shallow dish or a resealable plastic bag.
- Pour the rhubarb marinade over the protein, making sure it is well coated.
- Cover the dish or seal the bag, and refrigerate for at least 1 hour, or ideally overnight, to let the flavors infuse.

6. Cook Your Dish:

- Remove the protein from the marinade and discard any excess marinade.
- Grill, bake, or sauté the protein until cooked through, using the marinade as a glaze or basting sauce during cooking if desired.

Tips:

- Adjust the sweetness and saltiness of the marinade to your taste by adding more honey (or maple syrup) or soy sauce as needed.
- This rhubarb marinade is versatile and can be used for marinating a variety of dishes, from meats to tofu and vegetables.
- Store any leftover marinade in a sealed container in the refrigerator for up to one week. Use it as a sauce or glaze for other meals throughout the week.

Enjoy the tangy and flavorful twist that rhubarb marinade adds to your favorite dishes!

**Rhubarb Custard Bars**

Ingredients:

For the Crust:

- 1 1/2 cups all-purpose flour
- 1/2 cup powdered sugar
- 3/4 cup unsalted butter, softened

For the Rhubarb Layer:

- 3 cups chopped rhubarb (about 1/2-inch pieces)
- 1/2 cup granulated sugar
- 2 tablespoons water
- 1 tablespoon cornstarch

For the Custard Layer:

- 1 cup granulated sugar
- 1/4 cup all-purpose flour
- 1/2 teaspoon salt
- 2 large eggs
- 1/2 cup sour cream
- 1 teaspoon vanilla extract

Instructions:

1. Preheat the Oven:

- Preheat your oven to 350°F (175°C). Grease a 9x13-inch baking dish or line it with parchment paper.

2. Make the Crust:

- In a mixing bowl, combine the flour, powdered sugar, and softened butter.
- Use a pastry cutter or fork to blend the mixture until it resembles coarse crumbs.
- Press the mixture evenly into the bottom of the prepared baking dish.
- Bake the crust for 15 minutes in the preheated oven.

3. Prepare the Rhubarb Layer:

- In a saucepan, combine the chopped rhubarb, granulated sugar, and water.
- Cook over medium heat, stirring occasionally, until the rhubarb starts to break down and become tender, about 8-10 minutes.
- In a small bowl, mix the cornstarch with a tablespoon of water to create a slurry.
- Stir the cornstarch slurry into the rhubarb mixture and cook for another 1-2 minutes until thickened.
- Remove from heat and let the rhubarb mixture cool slightly.

4. Make the Custard Layer:

- In a mixing bowl, whisk together the granulated sugar, flour, and salt.
- Add the eggs, sour cream, and vanilla extract to the sugar mixture.
- Whisk until smooth and well combined.

5. Assemble the Bars:

- Spread the cooked rhubarb mixture evenly over the baked crust.
- Pour the custard mixture over the rhubarb layer, spreading it gently with a spatula to cover the rhubarb.

6. Bake and Cool:

- Bake the bars in the preheated oven for 35-40 minutes or until the custard is set and the edges are golden brown.
- Remove from the oven and let the bars cool completely in the baking dish on a wire rack.

7. Chill and Serve:

- Once cooled, refrigerate the bars for at least 2 hours or until chilled and set.
- Cut into squares and serve. Optionally, dust with powdered sugar before serving.

Enjoy these delicious rhubarb custard bars as a sweet and tangy dessert that's perfect for spring and summer gatherings!

**Rhubarb Lemon Bars**

Ingredients:

For the Crust:

- 1 cup all-purpose flour
- 1/4 cup powdered sugar
- 1/2 cup unsalted butter, softened

For the Rhubarb Lemon Filling:

- 2 cups chopped rhubarb (about 1/2-inch pieces)
- 1 cup granulated sugar
- Zest of 1 lemon
- 3 tablespoons fresh lemon juice
- 3 large eggs
- 1/4 cup all-purpose flour
- 1/2 teaspoon baking powder
- Powdered sugar, for dusting (optional)

Instructions:

1. Preheat the Oven:

- Preheat your oven to 350°F (175°C). Grease an 8x8-inch baking dish or line it with parchment paper.

2. Make the Crust:

- In a mixing bowl, combine the flour, powdered sugar, and softened butter.
- Use a pastry cutter or fork to blend the mixture until it resembles coarse crumbs.
- Press the mixture evenly into the bottom of the prepared baking dish.
- Bake the crust for 15 minutes in the preheated oven.

3. Prepare the Rhubarb Lemon Filling:

- In a saucepan, combine the chopped rhubarb, granulated sugar, lemon zest, and lemon juice.
- Cook over medium heat, stirring occasionally, until the rhubarb breaks down and becomes tender, about 8-10 minutes.
- Remove from heat and let the rhubarb mixture cool slightly.

4. Make the Lemon Filling:

- In a mixing bowl, whisk together the eggs, flour, and baking powder until smooth.
- Gradually whisk the rhubarb mixture into the egg mixture until well combined.

5. Assemble and Bake the Bars:

- Pour the lemon-rhubarb filling over the baked crust, spreading it evenly.
- Return the baking dish to the oven and bake for an additional 25-30 minutes or until the filling is set and the edges are lightly golden.
- Remove from the oven and let the bars cool completely in the baking dish on a wire rack.

6. Chill and Serve:

- Once cooled, refrigerate the bars for at least 2 hours or until chilled and firm.
- Dust with powdered sugar before slicing into squares and serving.

Enjoy these tangy and refreshing rhubarb lemon bars as a delightful dessert or treat for any occasion! The combination of rhubarb and lemon creates a perfect balance of sweet and tart flavors.

**Rhubarb Butter**

Ingredients:

- 4 cups chopped rhubarb (about 1/2-inch pieces)
- 1 cup granulated sugar
- 1/4 cup water
- Zest and juice of 1 lemon
- 1 cinnamon stick (optional)

Instructions:

1. Cook the Rhubarb:

- In a large saucepan, combine the chopped rhubarb, sugar, water, lemon zest, lemon juice, and cinnamon stick (if using).
- Cook over medium heat, stirring occasionally, until the rhubarb begins to break down and become soft, about 10-15 minutes.

2. Simmer and Reduce:

- Reduce the heat to low and continue to simmer the mixture, stirring occasionally, until it thickens and the rhubarb is completely softened, about 30-40 minutes.
- If using a cinnamon stick, remove it from the mixture once the desired flavor has infused.

3. Blend the Mixture:

- Remove the cooked rhubarb mixture from heat and let it cool slightly.
- Transfer the mixture to a blender or food processor.
- Blend until smooth and creamy. Alternatively, you can use an immersion blender directly in the saucepan.

4. Store or Serve:

- Pour the rhubarb butter into clean, sterilized jars or containers.
- Let it cool completely before sealing.
- Store in the refrigerator for up to 2 weeks.

Tips:

- Adjust the sweetness by adding more or less sugar, depending on your preference and the tartness of the rhubarb.
- Feel free to customize the flavor by adding spices like cinnamon, ginger, or vanilla extract.
- Rhubarb butter can be used in various ways: spread it on toast or biscuits, swirl it into yogurt or oatmeal, use it as a filling for tarts or pastries, or drizzle it over ice cream or pancakes.

Enjoy this delightful rhubarb butter and experiment with different ways to incorporate its unique flavor into your favorite dishes and treats!

**Rhubarb Crisp Bars**

Ingredients:

For the Rhubarb Filling:

- 4 cups chopped rhubarb (about 1/2-inch pieces)
- 1 cup granulated sugar
- 2 tablespoons cornstarch
- Zest and juice of 1 orange (optional)

For the Oat Crust and Topping:

- 1 1/2 cups old-fashioned rolled oats
- 1 1/2 cups all-purpose flour
- 1 cup packed brown sugar
- 1/2 teaspoon baking powder
- 1/4 teaspoon salt
- 1 cup unsalted butter, melted

Instructions:

1. Preheat the Oven:

- Preheat your oven to 350°F (175°C). Grease a 9x13-inch baking dish or line it with parchment paper.

2. Make the Rhubarb Filling:

- In a large bowl, combine the chopped rhubarb, granulated sugar, cornstarch, and orange zest and juice (if using). Toss to coat the rhubarb evenly.
- Let the rhubarb mixture sit for about 10 minutes to macerate and release some of its juices.

3. Prepare the Oat Crust and Topping:

- In a separate mixing bowl, combine the rolled oats, flour, brown sugar, baking powder, and salt.

- Pour in the melted butter and stir until the mixture is crumbly and well combined.

4. Assemble the Bars:

    - Press about two-thirds of the oat mixture evenly into the bottom of the prepared baking dish to form the crust.
    - Spoon the rhubarb filling over the oat crust, spreading it out evenly.

5. Add the Oat Topping:

    - Sprinkle the remaining oat mixture evenly over the rhubarb filling to form the crisp topping.

6. Bake and Serve:

    - Bake in the preheated oven for 40-45 minutes or until the topping is golden brown and the rhubarb filling is bubbling.
    - Remove from the oven and let the rhubarb crisp bars cool completely in the baking dish on a wire rack.
    - Once cooled, cut into squares or bars.

7. Serve and Enjoy:

    - Serve the rhubarb crisp bars at room temperature or slightly warmed, optionally with a scoop of vanilla ice cream on top.

Tips:

- You can add other fruits like strawberries or raspberries to the rhubarb filling for added flavor and color.
- Feel free to adjust the sweetness of the filling by adding more or less sugar, depending on your taste and the tartness of the rhubarb.
- Store any leftover bars in an airtight container at room temperature for up to 2 days, or in the refrigerator for longer shelf life.

These rhubarb crisp bars are a wonderful way to showcase the bright and tangy flavor of rhubarb in a delightful dessert. Enjoy!

**Rhubarb Baked Beans**

Ingredients:

- 1 pound dried navy beans or white beans, soaked overnight and drained
- 2 cups chopped rhubarb (about 1/2-inch pieces)
- 1 onion, finely chopped
- 3 cloves garlic, minced
- 1/2 cup ketchup
- 1/4 cup molasses
- 1/4 cup brown sugar
- 2 tablespoons Dijon mustard
- 2 tablespoons apple cider vinegar
- 1 teaspoon Worcestershire sauce
- 1/2 teaspoon smoked paprika (optional)
- Salt and pepper, to taste
- Water or vegetable broth, as needed

Instructions:

1. Precook the Beans:

- In a large pot, cover the soaked and drained beans with water or vegetable broth.
- Bring to a boil, then reduce heat and simmer for 30-40 minutes or until the beans are tender but still hold their shape.
- Drain and set aside.

2. Prepare the Rhubarb Mixture:

- In a saucepan, combine the chopped rhubarb, onion, garlic, ketchup, molasses, brown sugar, Dijon mustard, apple cider vinegar, Worcestershire sauce, smoked paprika (if using), salt, and pepper.
- Cook over medium heat, stirring occasionally, until the rhubarb breaks down and becomes tender, about 8-10 minutes.
- If the mixture becomes too thick, add a little water or vegetable broth to reach a saucy consistency.

3. Combine and Bake:

- Preheat your oven to 350°F (175°C).
- In a large mixing bowl, combine the cooked beans with the rhubarb mixture.
- Mix well to coat the beans evenly with the sauce.
- Transfer the bean mixture to a baking dish or casserole dish.

4. Bake:

- Cover the baking dish with foil and bake in the preheated oven for 45-60 minutes, or until the beans are bubbling and the flavors have melded together.
- Remove the foil during the last 15 minutes of baking to allow the top to brown slightly.

5. Serve and Enjoy:

- Serve the rhubarb baked beans hot as a side dish or main course.
- Garnish with fresh herbs like parsley or chives, if desired.

Tips:

- Adjust the sweetness and tanginess of the beans by varying the amount of brown sugar, molasses, and vinegar to suit your taste.
- Feel free to add diced bacon or ham for a smoky flavor, or smoked tofu for a vegetarian version.
- Leftover rhubarb baked beans can be stored in the refrigerator for up to 3-4 days. Reheat before serving.

These rhubarb baked beans are a flavorful and comforting dish that's perfect for gatherings or weeknight meals. Enjoy the unique combination of savory beans with the tartness of rhubarb!

**Rhubarb Coffee Cake**

Ingredients:

For the Cake:

- 2 cups chopped rhubarb (about 1/2-inch pieces)
- 1 1/2 cups granulated sugar
- 1/2 cup unsalted butter, softened
- 2 large eggs
- 1 teaspoon vanilla extract
- 2 cups all-purpose flour
- 1 teaspoon baking powder
- 1/2 teaspoon baking soda
- 1/4 teaspoon salt
- 1 cup sour cream or Greek yogurt

For the Crumb Topping:

- 1/2 cup all-purpose flour
- 1/2 cup packed brown sugar
- 1/4 cup unsalted butter, softened
- 1/2 teaspoon ground cinnamon

Instructions:

1. Preheat the Oven:

- Preheat your oven to 350°F (175°C). Grease a 9x13-inch baking dish or line it with parchment paper.

2. Prepare the Rhubarb:

- In a bowl, toss the chopped rhubarb with 1/2 cup of granulated sugar. Set aside while preparing the cake batter.

3. Make the Cake Batter:

- In a large mixing bowl, cream together the softened butter and remaining 1 cup of granulated sugar until light and fluffy.
- Add the eggs, one at a time, beating well after each addition.
- Stir in the vanilla extract.
- In a separate bowl, whisk together the flour, baking powder, baking soda, and salt.
- Gradually add the dry ingredients to the butter mixture, alternating with the sour cream (or Greek yogurt), beginning and ending with the flour mixture. Mix until just combined.

4. Assemble the Cake:

- Spread half of the cake batter into the prepared baking dish.
- Sprinkle the rhubarb mixture evenly over the batter.
- Spoon the remaining cake batter over the rhubarb layer, spreading it gently to cover the rhubarb.

5. Make the Crumb Topping:

- In a small bowl, combine the flour, brown sugar, softened butter, and cinnamon.
- Use a fork or pastry cutter to mix the ingredients until crumbly.
- Sprinkle the crumb topping evenly over the cake batter.

6. Bake and Serve:

- Bake in the preheated oven for 40-45 minutes or until a toothpick inserted into the center of the cake comes out clean.
- Remove the cake from the oven and let it cool in the baking dish on a wire rack for at least 20 minutes before serving.

7. Serve and Enjoy:

- Cut the rhubarb coffee cake into squares and serve warm or at room temperature.
- This cake is delicious on its own or served with a dollop of whipped cream or vanilla ice cream.

Enjoy this moist and flavorful rhubarb coffee cake as a delightful treat for breakfast, brunch, or dessert! The combination of tangy rhubarb and sweet crumb topping is sure to be a hit.

**Rhubarb Whiskey Sour**

Ingredients:

- 2 oz whiskey (bourbon or rye)
- 1 oz rhubarb syrup (recipe below)
- 3/4 oz fresh lemon juice
- Ice
- Rhubarb stalk or lemon twist, for garnish

For the Rhubarb Syrup:

- 2 cups chopped rhubarb (about 1/2-inch pieces)
- 1 cup granulated sugar
- 1 cup water

Instructions:

1. Make the Rhubarb Syrup:

- In a saucepan, combine the chopped rhubarb, granulated sugar, and water.
- Bring the mixture to a boil over medium-high heat, stirring occasionally to dissolve the sugar.
- Reduce the heat to low and simmer for about 10-15 minutes, or until the rhubarb is soft and the mixture has thickened slightly.
- Remove from heat and let the syrup cool.
- Strain the syrup through a fine mesh sieve to remove the solids.
- Store the rhubarb syrup in a sealed container in the refrigerator until ready to use.

2. Prepare the Rhubarb Whiskey Sour:

- In a cocktail shaker, combine the whiskey, rhubarb syrup, and fresh lemon juice.
- Fill the shaker with ice.
- Shake vigorously for about 15-20 seconds to chill the mixture.

3. Strain and Serve:

- Fill a rocks glass with ice.

- Strain the shaken mixture into the glass over the ice.
- Garnish with a rhubarb stalk or a twist of lemon peel.

4. Enjoy:

- Sip and enjoy your Rhubarb Whiskey Sour!

Tips:

- Adjust the sweetness and tartness of the cocktail by varying the amount of rhubarb syrup and lemon juice to suit your taste.
- You can experiment with different types of whiskey to find your preferred flavor profile for this cocktail.
- If you prefer a stronger rhubarb flavor, you can increase the amount of rhubarb syrup used in the cocktail.

This Rhubarb Whiskey Sour is a delightful and unique cocktail that's perfect for enjoying during the spring and summer months. The tangy rhubarb syrup adds a refreshing twist to the classic whiskey sour. Cheers!

**Rhubarb Fritters**

Ingredients:

For the Rhubarb Fritters:

- 2 cups chopped rhubarb (about 1/2-inch pieces)
- 1 cup all-purpose flour
- 2 tablespoons granulated sugar
- 1 teaspoon baking powder
- 1/4 teaspoon salt
- 1/2 cup milk (or buttermilk)
- 1 large egg
- 1 teaspoon vanilla extract
- Oil for frying (such as vegetable oil or canola oil)

For Dusting:

- Powdered sugar for dusting (optional)

Instructions:

1. Prepare the Rhubarb:

- Rinse and chop the rhubarb into small pieces (about 1/2-inch in size). Set aside.

2. Make the Batter:

- In a mixing bowl, whisk together the flour, granulated sugar, baking powder, and salt.
- In another bowl, whisk together the milk, egg, and vanilla extract.
- Pour the wet ingredients into the dry ingredients and mix until just combined. The batter should be thick and smooth.

3. Add the Rhubarb:

- Gently fold the chopped rhubarb into the batter until evenly distributed.

4. Fry the Fritters:

- In a heavy-bottomed pot or deep skillet, heat about 2 inches of oil over medium heat until it reaches 350°F (175°C).
- Using a spoon or a small ice cream scoop, carefully drop spoonfuls of the rhubarb batter into the hot oil, making sure not to overcrowd the pot.
- Fry the fritters for 2-3 minutes on each side or until they are golden brown and crispy.
- Use a slotted spoon or tongs to transfer the cooked fritters to a plate lined with paper towels to drain excess oil.
- Continue frying the remaining batter in batches.

5. Serve and Enjoy:

- Dust the rhubarb fritters with powdered sugar, if desired, before serving.
- Enjoy the fritters warm as a delightful dessert or snack.

Tips:

- Be careful when frying the fritters to maintain a consistent oil temperature. If the oil is too hot, the fritters may burn on the outside before cooking through. If it's too cool, they may absorb too much oil.
- You can customize the flavor of the fritters by adding spices like cinnamon or nutmeg to the batter.
- Serve the rhubarb fritters with a dollop of whipped cream or a scoop of vanilla ice cream for an extra special treat.

These rhubarb fritters are a delightful way to enjoy the seasonal flavor of rhubarb. The crispy exterior and tender, tart interior make them a perfect indulgence for any occasion!

**Rhubarb Cinnamon Rolls**

Ingredients:

For the Dough:

- 1 cup milk
- 1/4 cup unsalted butter, cubed
- 1/4 cup granulated sugar
- 2 1/4 teaspoons (1 packet) active dry yeast
- 3 1/4 cups all-purpose flour, plus more for dusting
- 1/2 teaspoon salt
- 1 large egg

For the Filling:

- 1 1/2 cups finely chopped rhubarb
- 1/2 cup granulated sugar
- 1 teaspoon ground cinnamon
- Zest of 1 lemon (optional)
- 2 tablespoons unsalted butter, softened

For the Cream Cheese Frosting:

- 4 ounces cream cheese, softened
- 1/4 cup unsalted butter, softened
- 1 cup powdered sugar
- 1/2 teaspoon vanilla extract

Instructions:

1. Prepare the Dough:

- In a small saucepan, heat the milk and butter over low heat until the butter is melted. Remove from heat and let it cool until warm but not hot.
- In a large mixing bowl, dissolve the granulated sugar and yeast in the warm milk mixture. Let it sit for about 5-10 minutes until foamy.
- Add 3 cups of flour and the salt to the yeast mixture. Stir until a dough forms.
- Transfer the dough to a lightly floured surface and knead for about 5-7 minutes, adding more flour as needed, until the dough is smooth and elastic.

- Place the dough in a greased bowl, cover with a clean kitchen towel or plastic wrap, and let it rise in a warm place for about 1-1.5 hours, or until doubled in size.

2. Make the Filling:

- In a small bowl, combine the chopped rhubarb, granulated sugar, cinnamon, and lemon zest (if using). Set aside.
- Once the dough has risen, punch it down and roll it out on a lightly floured surface into a large rectangle, about 16x12 inches.
- Spread the softened butter evenly over the dough, leaving a 1-inch border around the edges.
- Evenly distribute the rhubarb filling over the buttered dough.

3. Roll and Cut the Rolls:

- Starting from one of the long edges, tightly roll up the dough into a log.
- Use a sharp knife to cut the log into 12 equal slices.

4. Arrange and Bake:

- Place the slices in a greased 9x13-inch baking dish, cut-side up.
- Cover the dish with a clean kitchen towel or plastic wrap and let the rolls rise for another 30-45 minutes, until puffy.
- Meanwhile, preheat your oven to 375°F (190°C).
- Bake the rhubarb cinnamon rolls for 25-30 minutes, or until golden brown.

5. Make the Cream Cheese Frosting:

- While the rolls are baking, prepare the cream cheese frosting. In a mixing bowl, beat together the softened cream cheese and butter until smooth.
- Gradually add the powdered sugar and vanilla extract, beating until creamy and well combined.

6. Frost and Serve:

- Allow the cinnamon rolls to cool slightly before spreading the cream cheese frosting over the tops.
- Serve warm and enjoy your delicious rhubarb cinnamon rolls!

Tips:

- You can customize the filling by adding chopped nuts, raisins, or additional spices like nutmeg or cardamom.
- If you prefer a thinner frosting, add a tablespoon or two of milk to the cream cheese frosting mixture.
- These rhubarb cinnamon rolls are best enjoyed fresh but can be stored in an airtight container at room temperature for a day or two. Reheat them in the microwave briefly before serving if desired.

These rhubarb cinnamon rolls are sure to be a hit with their sweet, tangy filling and creamy frosting. They make a wonderful treat for breakfast, brunch, or dessert!

www.ingramcontent.com/pod-product-compliance
Lightning Source LLC
LaVergne TN
LVHW081556060526
838201LV00054B/1918